T0356308

STOP ME
IF I SAY
SOMETHING
CRAZY.

DISINFORMATION & DISSENT
IN THE POST-TRUTH WORLD

JOHN SCHONEBOOM

STOP ME IF I SAY SOMETHING CRAZY: DISINFORMATION & DISSENT IN THE POST-TRUTH WORLD.
COPYRIGHT © 2024/2025. JOHN SCHONEBOOM. ALL RIGHTS RESERVED.

Published by:
Trine Day LLC
PO Box 577
Walterville, OR 97489
1-800-556-2012
www.TrineDay.com
trineday@icloud.com

Library of Congress Control Number: 2025930615

Schoneboom, John. STOP ME IF I SAY SOMETHING CRAZY—1st ed.
p. cm.

Epub (ISBN-13) 978-1-63424-510-4
Trade Paper (ISBN-13) 978-1-63424-509-8

1. Technology and state. 2. Freedom of speech. 3. Dissenters. 4. Social media Political aspects United States. 5. Truthfulness and falsehood United States. 6. Propaganda. 7. Disinformation United States. 8. Social media and society United States. I. Schoneboom, John. II. Title.

FIRST EDITION
10 9 8 7 6 5 4 3 2 1

Distribution to the Trade by:
Independent Publishers Group (IPG)
814 North Franklin Street
Chicago, Illinois 60610
312.337.0747
www.ipgbook.com

Apparently there is no limit, Joe remarked. Anything can be said in this place and it will be true and will have to be believed.

– Flann O'Brien
The Third Policeman

The deception of whole peoples is not a matter which can be lightly regarded.

–Arthur Ponsonby
Falsehood in Time of War

CONTENTS

INTRODUCTION

What do you do with dissent when there's no time for it because it's an emergency, but you live in a democracy that supposedly values debate? It's complicated! Take the Covid crisis, for example, which arrived with all sorts of unknowns begging for educated opinions and all sorts of rules begging for unwavering compliance. What do you do when some of the educated opinions are at odds with the unwavering compliance? Something's got to give.

Stanford University physician Jay Bhattacharya tweets statistical data showing that Covid almost exclusively threatens the elderly.

Twitter blacklists him.[1]

Another Stanford University physician, John Ioannidis, one of the world's leading epidemiologists, argues that the Covid response should be informed by data and questions the wisdom of the lockdowns.

YouTube removes the video.[2]

At a United States Senate committee hearing, Dr. Pierre Kory, Critical Care Service Chief at University of Wisconsin School of Medicine and Public Health, presents evidence of early treatment protocols having success against Covid in large-scale programs in India, Argentina, Peru, and elsewhere.

YouTube removes the video – a video of a Senate hearing.[3]

Dr. Robert Malone, a contributor to the invention of mRNA vaccine technology, calls for caution, saying the platform he helped create came with certain dangers.

Twitter bans him.[4]

Dr. Martin Kulldorff, Professor of Medicine at Harvard University and member of the CDC Covid-19 Vaccine Safety Technical Work Group, argues *in favor* of the J&J vaccine, saying it's safe to continue giving it to older people, after the CDC decided to suspend it for everyone. He also argues *against* vaccine mandates, particularly for those with natural immunity from prior infection.

For the former opinion, he is fired from the CDC. For the latter, he is fired from Harvard.[5]

Dr. Meryl Nass treats her Covid patients with ivermectin and criticizes her state governor's Covid policies on a radio program. Her patients do well; none are harmed; none complain.

At the behest of the governor's sister, the Maine medical board suspends Dr. Nass's medical license.[6]

An analysis of 325 post-vaccine autopsy findings by a team of highly regarded experts, including Harvey Risch, Yale University's Professor Emeritus of epidemiology, is posted on *The Lancet*'s preprint server.

The Lancet abruptly withdraws the paper before peer review.[7] The paper subsequently does get peer reviewed elsewhere and is published by the Elsevier journal *Forensic Science International*, where it becomes the top trending research paper worldwide across all subject areas, according to the Observatory of International Research,[8] only to be withdrawn and completely wiped from the journal's server a few weeks later following anonymous complaints.[9]

Dr. Peter McCullough, Consultant Cardiologist and Vice Chair of Internal Medicine at Baylor University Medical Center, with over a thousand peer-reviewed publications, argues that there is no medical reason for people with natural immunity from prior Covid infection to get the jab, and accurately notes the number of deaths reported in the CDC's own vaccine safety monitoring system, which makes no claims as to causality but is intended to signal potential problems.

The American Board of Internal Medicine – which relies on Dr. McCullough's publications for some of its educational and testing content – revokes his certification.[10]

These are just a few examples of what was evidently a concerted and uncompromising effort to manage information around Covid. Countless others could be listed.

Some will feel that this information-control program was a responsible public health intervention to save lives by minimizing dangerous disinformation and misinformation. Others will feel it was inappropriate censorship that not only ran contrary to democratic and scientific principles but was ultimately counterproductive to public health goals.

A person on either side of that divide could, would, and did call those on the other side "anti-science." The nice thing about that is that science has ways of showing who's got the better argument. We'll be taking a close look at some of those ways in theory and practice.

This book will neither advocate nor vilify any particular positions, because what am I, a doctor, a scientist, an engineer? Nope, nope, and nope.

This book is about methods, which we can all understand. It's about the process by which we arrive at positions.

My starting point – my bias – centers on the principle that heterodox views and the debates that they entail are the lifeblood of both science and democracy. There are undoubtedly limits to that principle, but first things first. How is truth determined? Does a position become an orthodoxy by force of evidence or by evidence of force? We can test for that — by looking at the process.

In order to function, science and democracy both *need* competing ideas and transparent processes. One can't simply assert and demand; one must demonstrate and persuade. Yet, as we can see in the examples above, complex new issues that would seemingly invite thoughtful discussion and informed debate are instead almost instantly triaged into required and forbidden views – an absolutist binary in the mold of the "with us or against us" declaration with which George W. Bush launched the age of the permanent emergency.[11]

We do literally live in a state of permanent emergency, by the way, at least in the United States. It's official. Proclamation 7463 was declared after September 11, 2001, because of "the continuing and immediate threat of further attacks." It has been renewed annually ever since, by Democrat and Republican alike, spilling into putative domestic threats,[12] whittling away at civil liberties,[13] and by all appearances metastasizing into a general-purpose with-us-or-against-us mindset that exists in tension with democratic principles. Along with required and forbidden opinions comes the division of society into seemingly irreconcilable factions faced off in deep mutual disdain.

In the paradigm of the absolutist binary, transgressive views are considered not just incorrect, but literally intolerable. Proving dissent wrong would require something unacceptable: intellectual engagement. Dismissing it requires only pointing and laughing. Since not being a ridiculous laughingstock ranks pretty highly among most people's life goals, turning dissent into shame — tabooing dissent, in other words — is a highly effective deterrent. The required views are thereby shielded from serious scrutiny.

Thus the absolutist binary isn't just about identifying friends and enemies, it's also about terrifying people into conformity. Views on the wrong side of that binary can be met with severe social, professional, and financial consequences.[14] Goodbye hypotheses, data, forensic techniques, and peer review. Hello "On Narrative" (with us, intelligent, good, sane) and "Off Narrative" (against us, evil, stupid, mad).

It isn't just Covid. Court cases[15] and other documents[16] have demonstrated that media companies (social and otherwise) have actively established required and forbidden views on many thorny issues, from foreign wars to election interference, often at the behest of government agencies.[17] Of course, the official response is that agency actions aren't about squashing dissent or restricting anybody's legitimate free speech rights — they're about dealing with dangerous disinformation in the midst of a crisis.

The question is: Without dissent, discussion, and debate, how do you know it's disinformation?

The lab-leak theory of Covid's origins was initially denounced in the most withering possible terms as a contemptible conspiracy theory from the lunatic fringe. A person could get kicked off social media for suggesting the idea. Then it emerged that the FBI, the Defense Intelligence Agency, and the Department of Energy each assessed it to be a credible if not likely explanation.[18] Hunter Biden's famous laptop with its cache of incriminating documents was pure Russian disinformation according to the consensus of 51 former intelligence officials — 51, count 'em – until it was confirmed to be authentic after all.[19]

One might be tempted to make the argument that these turnabouts indicate that there's no problem, that the system is working: "When they get things wrong, they're soon corrected." Sometimes. However, the point isn't that they got things wrong. It's that they demonized dissent. The lab-leak theory might still be wrong, but it should never have been deemed a forbidden thought.

Demonization of dissent is an anti-democratic, anti-scientific practice that delays and at times surely prevents the determination of truth. It's also the single most defining characteristic of a dystopian society. Ask any science fiction writer.

It is therefore this tabooing of dissent that draws our scrutiny. It indicates that the normal, desirable procedures of science and democracy have been suspended. It has proven, at least sometimes, to correlate with unreliable official narratives. And, as John Stuart Mill put it in *On Liberty*: "All silencing of discussion is an assumption of infallibility."[20] And as we've seen, the would-be Ministers of Truth, like everyone else, are far from infallible.

So if an official narrative is being heavily promoted and dissent around it is tabooed as disinformation, maybe it's worth a closer look on general principle. Maybe the dissent really *is* disinformation. Maybe it's not. Maybe the word disinformation is being used as disinformation. How can we tell?

An obvious difficulty for us as lay people is that understanding whether something is disinformation or not often requires expertise that is far beyond our capabilities. We don't know who did or didn't commit a chemical attack. We weren't there. We didn't even receive any of the soil samples. We don't know whether a cheap generic medicine is as good or better than a profitable patented new drug. We don't know how to begin to navigate the specialized terrain of clinical trials, observational studies, conflicts of interest, or corporate capture of nominal regulators.

All we know usually is that somebody is offering evidence of something. Should we believe it? Is it accurate? Does it mean what they say it means? Is there missing context? Were there unstated conflicts of interest or built-in biases? Are there valid counter-arguments?

Who the hell knows! We know we want assertions to be backed by evidence, but it turns out evidence isn't often of much use to us. So how can we navigate this minefield of science, pseudo-science, lunacy, and bullshit? Trust the experts and fact checkers? Which ones? Sponsored by whom? We desperately need a reliable way involving our own thinking to tell reality from delusion in the post-truth world. That's why we'll focus not on evidence we can't evaluate, but on methods we can.

Truth may fail, but lies leave a trail.

Nonsense is detectable. We can tell when there's a rabbit off because we know what's supposed to happen and not happen in science. The scientific method comes with certain standard expectations: empiricism, transparency, reproducibility, independent analysis, and the need to account for all of the evidence. It involves the welcoming of multiple hypotheses in order to avoid confirmation bias. It is explicitly opposed to political and religious dogma as barriers to the demonstration of truth.

There are other things the scientific method explicitly does *not* involve. It doesn't involve hiding, distorting, falsifying, inventing, ignoring, or cherry-picking data. It doesn't involve rigging studies to ensure a desired outcome. It doesn't involve accusing dissenters of heresy and demonetizing their YouTube channels.

These are the sorts of things we can fruitfully examine in order to get a better idea of the reliability of science-based positions on either side of a binary divide. We don't need to be subject experts. We're all capable of making judgements about a process when we know how it's generally supposed to go.

Let's practice.

There's a scientific dispute. One side says: "Your conclusion isn't consistent with the evidence we have right here. Please have a look and let's see if we can resolve the discrepancies."

If the other side comes back with "I see, I see — good heavens you're right, it's back to the drawing board!" or "Hmm, no, my friend, I'm afraid it's you who have made the mistake — you've miscalculated the Cabibbo angle!" — great. Either way. Science is happening.

But if the other side comes back with: "I'm calling the gestapo! Say goodbye to your fingernails!" — or with unsupported allegations, ad hominem attacks, or mindless pejoratives — then we're not talking science any more, are we? We still might not have the truth quite in hand, but we'll certainly have a scent to follow.

If a narrative is constructed with bad science, no matter how aggressively it is promoted, no matter how many people believe it, it will remain fundamentally flimsy.

The key to evaluating assertions, as Bertrand Russell has argued in his seminal treatise on propaganda,[21] is to develop a mental state of "critical undogmatic receptiveness," also known as an actively open mind. Before we can cultivate that elusive state, we mainly need one other thing first: We have to *care* whether things are true or not. I mean actually care.

Do we? It's not that easy. The usual thing is to go binary and keep to our own people: the stuff my people believe is true-good-sane, and the stuff those other people believe is false-evil-nuts. We're with us, and they're against us, and that's all we want to know. Whatever we want to believe, we know we can always find a link to some article that supports it. We know the other side can too, but their links are stupid and ours are real.

Wine and chocolate are good for me? It's true and I'm done researching. Those are my go-to studies. I'll point to them no matter what anyone else says. Are those things *really* true? I don't know. I don't *want* to know. They might be true. They're true enough for me to stop looking. They're true enough to maintain my happy place.

This is confirmation bias. Confirmation bias is trying to prove yourself right. Science – truth-seeking – is trying to prove yourself wrong.

As noted above, documents from the Twitter Files and other sources have revealed that government pressure on media plays an active role in narrative management. The hard-to-control online frontier of social media and alternative news sources seems to have driven the recent increased interest in more overt forms of censorship and propaganda than had previously been required.

Arm twisting isn't often necessary for the legacy media. Consent, as Noam Chomsky and Edward Herman have explained, is manufactured by culture.[22] It's the air we breathe. From early education through the mechanisms of career advancement, the culture "selects for obedience and subordination," as Chomsky told journalist Andrew Marr. When Marr objected that he himself as a BBC journalist could say anything he wanted, Chomsky famously replied: "I'm sure you believe everything you're saying. But what I'm saying is if you believed something different, you wouldn't be sitting where you're sitting."[23] No instructions, no conspiracy required.

This kind of cultural selection for obedience isn't just for journalists. It's for all of us. Narrative conformity is constantly reinforced as normal, good, intelligent, sane. Dissent is for morons and lunatics. These messages comprise what Lacan called the "symbolic order" of a culture, and (to varying degrees) we internalize them. Lacan's "big Other" is the figure that represents total internalization of all official narratives – the perfect non-transgressive consumer of PR and propaganda. Most real people diverge, at least privately, at least a little bit, and hold little shadow views that in turn hold some of the best potential for social change.

An internalized belief is one that doesn't need overt enforcement – or inspire rebellion. Examining narratives for truth content means allowing for the possibility that propaganda might not be something that only happens to other people. It means allowing for the possibility that some of our internalized beliefs about smart-sane and stupid-loony might be backwards. It means allowing for the possibility of deviating from one's tribe in a particular matter. It means having a bit of courage and a taste for adventure.

Why would we want to do that? We could start with President Eisenhower's unsettling farewell address, which he spent warning us about corruption from overly influential military, corporate, scientific, and technocratic elites, urging us to "take nothing for granted" because security and liberty can only be compelled by "an alert and knowledgeable citizenry."[24]

Our motivation also comes from the awareness that, while we certainly don't want to end up agreeing with any nut jobs or odious ideologues, we also don't want to end up being credulous suckers for authoritarian hucksters. Surely our safest, most bulletproof path is to do our best to make sure we're not buying any pigs in a poke from anybody. How do we do that? We listen to Bertrand Russell. We employ critical undogmatic receptiveness.

This book is going to try a bit of that. We'll examine controversial case studies where the official narrative is so tightly woven into the common-sense fabric of society that dissent is only for morons and lunatics. These are the issues where the case in favor of limits to free speech should be at its most compelling, where the dismissal of dissent as disinformation should be most clearly justified. These will be issues with science at the core, so that we can compare what did happen — how the competing positions were determined — with what we know should have happened: transparency, independent review, and competing justifiable hypotheses treated dispassionately in an honest search for truth.

The question we will try to answer is not which position is correct in any given case. Again: we're not subject experts. Rather, we're interested in the question of whether either or both positions have diverged from the normal procedures of science. If we can't tell, hey: toss a coin. Go with your people. If we *can* tell, well, hopefully any funny business isn't on the side we'd prefer to believe. If it is, we'll find ourselves at a crossroads. A crisis of intellect, and of conscience. It'll be exciting!

The looking-at-methods method should be able to go some way towards separating the wheat from the chaff. If the nut job position is nutty, it should show exactly why. If the official position doesn't hold up, it should show that too.

The idea is this: If even these universally derided positions can produce somewhere among them a single surprisingly sound argument in contrast to all the messaging, we'll have ample reason to interrogate the messengers. If the emperor has no clothes, we're going to need to have a serious conversation with all the townspeople who told us otherwise.

No futile attempt to hide authorial biases will be made, but the conclusions that can be drawn from this exercise will of course be your own (my own "conclusion" chapter notwithstanding). You might decide that all the right things have happened; the symbolic order has structural integrity and all we have to do is manage our disinformation nut jobs properly.

You might decide that, in at least some cases, we've strayed from the path of science and democracy. If that happens often enough, in important-enough ways, it might indicate that our society isn't quite what it says on the tin, that perhaps Eisenhower wasn't just being a big old drama queen. It might prove to be a good argument for slowing down and taking time for thought, discussion, debate, and democracy before we yield to knee-jerk binary absolutism with all its tribal divisiveness and potential for violence.

Bearing in mind all of the above, as you proceed through the rest of this slim volume I have just one request:

Stop me if I say something crazy.

A Chemical Attack

B
ack in 2018, the hot war du jour was in Syria. Various rebel groups, from the US-supported Free Syrian Army (which the US described as "moderate rebels")[25] to the notorious ISIS (which nobody described as moderate), were staging attacks and taking territory in an attempt to oust President Bashar al-Assad.

The town of Douma, near Damascus, had been under the control of a rebel faction known as Jaysh al-Islam, but Syria's forces were on the verge of chasing them out and securing the area. Syria was winning the war.[26] The only hope for the beleaguered rebels was that sympathetic Western governments might massively intervene on their behalf. That was unlikely, unless maybe Syria did something stupid, militarily unnecessary, and highly provocative like crossing the United States' "red line" by unleashing a chemical attack.[27]

On April 7 of that year, reports emerged of dozens of dead bodies, including many children, piled up inside a Douma apartment building, many of them frothing at the mouth and nose. Something appeared to have killed them almost instantly; a clear, handy exit path went untaken, meaning they must simply not have had time to escape.

The United States, United Kingdom, and France launched punitive missile strikes against Syria within the week. And then, in a reversal of the logical order of events, literally as the missiles were striking, a forensic investigation by the Organization for the Prohibition of Chemical Weapons (OPCW) began.

To the presumed relief of the punitive-missile-launching coalition, the OPCW's final report concluded that the dead bodies were the result of chemical weapons delivered via canisters dropped through the roof by helicopter, with the obvious implication the attack was ordered by Assad (a subsequent OPCW report four years later connected the final dot and directly accused Assad[28]).

The candidate chemicals were sarin (a nerve agent) or chlorine. Sarin, initially thought to be the more likely because of the observed results, e.g., the foaming at the mouth and apparent immediacy of death, was ruled out early because OPCW investigators found no trace of it at the scene or in biomedical samples.[29] That left chlorine.

The problem with chlorine gas was that, unlike a nerve gas, it wouldn't kill instantly and drop people where they stood. It wouldn't cause them to foam at the mouth. But there were traces of chlorine, so chlorine it was.

If you look it up on Wikipedia, you'll find the unambiguous conclusion: Assad used molecular chlorine on an apartment building in Douma.[30]

You could be forgiven for assuming that this conclusion about Assad using chemical weapons came from the OPCW Fact-Finding Mission (FFM) that went to Douma to investigate the matter. Strangely enough, you'd be wrong.

We know from leaked documents and the testimony of two important whistleblowers, senior members of the FFM team — Brendan Whelan[31] (a PhD chemist with 17 years' experience with OPCW, responsible for sampling and analysis) and Ian Henderson[32] (a chemical engineer and experienced OPCW trainer and team leader with a military background in artillery and weapons systems development) — that the consensus report of the Douma FFM team was that there was no evidence of a chemical attack.

I beg your pardon?

Chlorinated organic compounds (COCs) were indeed found, but levels were no higher than one would expect to find in any household environment and could in no way be said to indicate a poison gas attack. The team consulted with German military toxicologists, whose report stated unequivocally that the victims did not die of chlorine poisoning. Furthermore, Henderson's engineering assessment was that the condition and locations of the canisters were not consistent with them being dropped through a roof, and that the only plausible explanation was that they had been manually placed there.[33] The unstated implication was that the rebels themselves had murdered the victims and staged the scene to blame Assad.

OPCW's interim report made such substantive changes to the original team's findings that its conclusions were "contrary to what had previously been agreed,"[34] according to Whelan's leaked letter to the Director-General.

Engineer Henderson testified that, upon objecting to the changes in the interim report, he was told by a mediator that "we have been told by the first floor [the Office of the Director General] that we have to make it sound like we found something."[35] After that, the original investigating team was called into a briefing by a three-person US delegation from an unspecified agency – I'm guessing they wore black suits and sunglasses – who instructed the team without offering new evidence that indeed it was a chemical weapons attack, and the chemical was chlorine. The team found the presentation to be unconvincing. And inappropriate. And weird.

Henderson received an email ordering him to "remove the [engineering assessment] document from the [OPCW archive], and remove all traces, if any, of its delivery and storage there."[36] The Head of Operations was instructed by the Chief of Cabinet not to read the assessment. Since Henderson was the only engineer working in this area, this behavior seemed doubly strange.

The result of the objections by Whelan, Henderson, and others was that the original Douma team, except for one paramedic, was taken off the project and replaced by a new team that had not gone to Douma. This new team, which OPCW called the "core team," would be responsible for writing the final report.

When the final report came out, the existence of detectable chlorine was reported without the context that it was at or below the normal expected background levels. Also missing from the final report was the unequivocal German toxicology report ruling out chlorine poisoning. The engineering assessment was ignored, but a contrary conclusion of three new anonymous engineers was inserted without supporting evidence. The final report made the assertion that there were "reasonable grounds" to believe "molecular chlorine" was used in Douma. The evidence and reasoning justifying that assertion were not explained.[37]

Henderson requested meetings, including with the Director-General, and notified the Office of Internal Oversight, with the hope of the original Douma team getting together with the new "core" team, so the new team could explain what new information had been uncovered or what new analysis had been performed, and to compare engineering notes with the three anonymous experts whose findings were the opposite of the Douma team's. As Henderson testified:

> "[I]t is the method of scientific rigour that dictates that one side cannot profess to be the sole owner of the truth. It should follow the tried and tested method of scientific debate and peer review, leading to consensus. This requires the three 'independent experts' to present and defend their work in a scientific/engineering forum, together with the same from myself. This should lead to an understanding of the differences and, hopefully, lead to consensus.

13

Should consensus not be reached, the next stage would be to assemble a panel of agreed impartial, suitably-qualified experts to assess the two competing views and to make a judgement. I have no doubt that this would successfully clarify what happened in Douma on 7 April 2018."[38]

In other words, this was a plea for normal science: full transparency in the comparison of the merits of competing hypotheses.

All his requests were denied. The responses he received included "this is too big"; "it's too late now"; "this would not be good for the [organization's] reputation"; "don't make yourself a martyr"; and "but this would play into the Russian narrative."[39]

These developments, to this point, occurred behind the closed doors of OPCW; the public was blissfully unaware. The leaking of some of the Douma team's objections changed that, and things turned even uglier. The inspectors were treated to an onslaught of ad hominem attacks and attempts to dismiss them as marginal figures and "disgruntled" employees.[40]

Fernando Arias, the OPCW Director-General, insisted: "[The inspectors] are not whistleblowers. They are individuals who could not accept that their views were not backed by evidence ... their conclusions are erroneous, uninformed, and wrong".[41] US ambassador to the UN Kelly Clark characterized the inspectors' story as a "desperate and failed attempt by Russia to further spread disinformation"[42]; Nicolas de Rivière, the French ambassador, also called it a "disinformation exercise"[43]; Jonathan Allen, the UK ambassador, sneered at Henderson's "so-called evidence".[44] A *Guardian* article taking the OPCW claims at face value called the investigators' attempts to defend their team's work "a Russia-led campaign" (Wintour and McKernan 2020).[45]

So. Do we know what the truth is here? What are we, chemical weapons specialists? No, we know nothing about the truth. We do know how science is supposed to work. And this is the UN we're talking about. The OPC-freakin-W. Not Joe Schmoe's Shady U-Pay-We-Say Reporting Agency. So did the OPCW follow normal scientific procedures in establishing and defending its conclusions about Douma?

Here's what we know. They kicked the on-the-ground investigators off the team when they didn't "make it sound like we found something." They contradicted the investigative team's conclusions without offering new analyses or new data and ditched their engineer's assessment in favor of a contrary new assessment by anonymous engineers, again without offering supporting explanations or data. They omitted contrary evidence. They ignored the pleas to compare and review the different conclusions, with outside independent experts if necessary. They vilified the investigative team with personal attacks.

They did, somehow, get "Russia" and "disinformation" into a conversation about long-serving, seemingly rather dedicated, principled, and decidedly not-Russian career scientists. The few journalists who covered the whistleblower side of this story were also attacked as Putin's useful idiots and all the usual with-us-or-against-us pejoratives.

Is this science, or does it sound more like politics? Has the Assad-did-a-chemical-attack narrative earned its place as an indisputable truth? What is the scientific basis for maligning the conclusions of the career scientists from OPCW as Russian disinformation? Was Henderson's plea to compare evidence using normal science maybe a good idea? Wouldn't that have been an ideal way to find out which conclusion was better supported? Isn't there, at the very least, an obviously legitimate case for further discussion instead of an absolutist binary of a good-sane-intelligent required view and an evil-lunatic-moron forbidden one?

I dunno. You decide. Let's try another one. Nothing too controversial. How about the collapse of Building 7 on September 11, 2001? That should be straightforward engineering stuff.

A COLLAPSING BUILDING

Well, we're stepping right in it now. Nut job central. We're going all the way back to September 11, 2001, to the nuttiest nut jobs in all of nut jobbery. Yes it's a little nostalgia trip back to the strange case of the swift, complete collapse of the 47-story World Trade Center (WTC) Building 7. Classic.

One must admit that it was *swift*: depending on when you start counting, it took 5 or 7 seconds from collapse initiation to completion, including at least 2.25 seconds of pure no-resistance-whatsoever free fall, according even to official government sources.[46]

One must admit it was *complete*: none of that building was left. It went straight down into its own footprint. No large pieces of concrete flooring or intact structural framing remained.

And one must admit it was *strange*: it was the first-ever instance of the complete collapse of a tall steel-framed building attributed purely to fire. If you haven't seen it, you really must go find a video.

Building 7 was not, of course, hit by an airplane. It did suffer debris damage from the collapse of WTC1, aka the North Tower, but according to the National Institute for Standards and Technology (NIST), which produced the government's final official explanatory report,[47] the damage was not a factor in the building's collapse. Fire, and fire alone, brought down this beast. How? Thermal expansion. We'll get to that.

We're going to end up comparing two computer models here, one from NIST and one from the University of Alaska Fairbanks, but we'll need a little context first. Let's take a deep breath, relax our shoulders, remain in serene good humor, and have a nice, calm, rational look at the fire hypothesis and its main competitor from nut job planet: controlled demolition.

This is obviously one where conspiracy theorists come out in droves, but we'll approach this exercise fairly with our usual open minds. NIST spent seven years and a lot of ingenuity figuring out what happened and we'll take a good look at what they came up with. We'll verify that they've followed sound scientific principles. Then we'll see if any of the criticisms hold any water. Please turn your critical undogmatic receptiveness mode on now.

I think we do have to be sympathetic to one point from the nut job side of things: the collapse of Building 7 certainly *looked like* a controlled demolition. We now know that it wasn't one, thanks to NIST. But one must concede the collapse's *appearance* is indistinguishable from a controlled demolition, as even commentators on network news remarked in real time as it happened.[48] It had all the key features: sudden onset; near-perfect symmetry; straight-down collapse avoiding damage to surrounding structures; near-free-fall speed. This much is undeniable and, indeed, undenied.

For all the considerable technical expertise that goes into achieving these key features on purpose, one can only marvel that random fires here and there on a few floors managed to produce the exact same effect by accident.

Not to belabor the point, but it wasn't just shell-shocked home viewers and news anchors who thought it looked like the controlled demolition that we now know it wasn't. It looked so much like a controlled demolition that even controlled demolition experts who spent their careers doing controlled demolitions were convinced that it was obviously a controlled demolition.

In 2006, Danny Jowenko, the owner of a controlled demolition company in the Netherlands, was shown a video of the Building 7 collapse without being told when it had happened. Asked what had happened to the building, Jowenko said: "They simply blew up columns, and the rest caved in afterwards…This is controlled demolition." When asked if he was certain, he replied: "Absolutely, it's been imploded. This was a hired job. A team of experts did this." He went very quiet when he was told it fell on September 11.[49]

So, just because NIST has shown that expert opinion to be wrong, none of us need to feel overly stupid for having thought it *looked* exactly like a controlled demolition. It even fooled Danny Jowenko, professional controlled demolisher.

A controlled demolition would imply, of course, a series of increasingly disturbing questions about complicity, access, planning, and so forth that I will leave the curious to ponder on their own. Fortunately NIST finally provided a scientific explanation that is not nearly as disturbing as the implied "inside job," although it does imply very serious inadequacies in building codes that persist unchanged to this day. It turns out that the miracle isn't that Building 7 fell, but that so far no other buildings have crumpled into a heap as a result of this newly discovered construction vulnerability, especially considering that so many high-rises have endured so many much-worse fires.

Before we recap the basics of NIST's explanation and methods, let's take a moment to appreciate how difficult the NIST scientists' job was, and how therefore heroic their efforts were. Since they ruled out controlled demolition from the very beginning, they had to answer the extremely difficult question: What, *other* than controlled demolition, could make a building collapse in a way that behaved exactly *like* controlled demolition? What unprecedented sequence of events might account for it? It's a tough one, which is undoubtedly why it took so many years to produce the answer. They weren't the first ones to attempt it either.

The Federal Emergency Management Agency (FEMA) was the first government outfit tasked with explaining the weirdness of Building 7. Not only did they fail, conceding that their best hypothesis — some tepid conjecture about diesel fuel maybe playing a role — had "only a low probability of occurrence," they also ended up highlighting an issue that made it even more difficult to explain: evaporated steel.[50]

You heard me. Evaporated steel.

The FEMA report included an appendix by three professors from Worcester Polytechnic Institute (WPI), which described a phenomenon that reporter James Glanz in *The New York Times* called "[p]erhaps the deepest mystery uncovered in the investigation."[51] A WPI publication explained:

> [S]teel – which has a melting point of 2,800 degrees Fahrenheit – may weaken and bend, but does not melt during an ordinary office fire. Yet metallurgical studies on WTC steel … reveal that … a eutectic reaction occurred at the surface, causing intergranular melting capable of turning a solid steel girder into Swiss cheese … A one-inch column has been reduced to half-inch thickness. Its edges – which are curled like a paper scroll – have been thinned to almost razor sharpness. Gaping holes – some larger than a silver dollar – let light shine through a formerly solid steel flange. This Swiss cheese appearance shocked all of the fire-wise professors, who expected to see distortion and bending – but not holes.[52]

In short, as Glanz put it, the steel had evidently "been partly evaporated in extraordinarily high temperatures."[53]

Meditate on that.

A eutectic reaction, incidentally, is one in which two or more solids combine into a substance that melts at a lower temperature than they would individually. In the case of the Building 7 steel, the FEMA report described a "sulfur-rich liquid" that "liquefied the steel" at temperatures approaching 1,000 degrees C (1,800 degrees F) . The FEMA appendix concludes with a call for more study, noting that this liquefaction of steel is "a very unusual event" and that there is "no clear explanation for the source of the sulfur."[54]

The nut jobs are quick to point out that one simple explanation would be thermate. Thermate is a powerful incendiary that adds sulfur to little-brother-incendiary thermite for improved penetration of target, making it highly suitable for demolition purposes. It can form the liquid eutectic that FEMA found had attacked the steel. It would explain the sulfur, the temperatures, the intergranular melting, the Swiss cheese, all the observable features of the entire collapse. As a scientific hypothesis, it's actually pretty perfect, except for one thing:

It's madder than a bag of badgers.

That's the problem NIST had with it. The agency has said that, having "investigated carefully," it does not believe thermite or thermate were used to sever columns in Building 7. Why not? Because a lot of it would have been required, and "it is unlikely" that the required amount could have been brought in and applied without someone saying hey, who are you suspicious-looking strangers and what are you doing in that elevator shaft?[55]

Seems reasonable. Still, did they test for it, just in case, just to be sure, just to arrive at their conclusion through science, just to bolster their reasonable intuition with data, just to rule it out definitively, just to silence the nut jobs once and for all? Or just because that's what you're supposed to do according to the National Fire Protection Association's *Guide for Fire and Explosion Investigations*, which stipulates that you must test for evidence of explosives whenever there's "high-order damage" like a completely pulverized building?[56]

Unfortunately not. Journalist Jennifer Abel of the *Hartford Advocate* asked NIST spokesman Michael Newman why the agency didn't look for evidence of explosives. Newman responded that they didn't look for it "because there was no evidence of that." Abel asked the obvious follow-up: "But how can you know there's no evidence if you don't look for it first?"

"If you're looking for something that isn't there," Newman responded, "you're wasting your time ... and the taxpayers' money."[57]

To be fair, Newman is not a scientist. Nor is he a comedian. He's a PR guy. He's doing his best, but he's out of his depth. Who can blame him for being irritable? He'll have been sweating. He probably couldn't wait to get out of there. Hopefully he didn't go home and kick his dog. Let's forgive him.

The other reason NIST gave for not looking for evidence of explosives was that "no blast sounds" of the expected volume were heard on audio-visual recordings or reported by witnesses.[58] There are certainly some startling bangs on some of the videos online, and former NYPD officer Craig Barmer did say he was "real close to Building 7" and that there was "a lot of eyewitness testimony down there of hearing explosions…the whole time you're hearing 'boom, boom, boom, boom, boom.'" Two men *inside* Building 7 in the morning both described an explosion that destroyed a landing as they raced down the stairs to get out, blowing them back and trapping them on the floor above; they had to be rescued through a window by firefighters.[59]

Sounds of course are subject to interpretation and misinterpretation and NIST obviously evaluated these things and determined that these explosive boom-booms were not likely to be blast sounds from explosions and the men inside were perhaps confused in the general chaos of the day.

The agency did include a single hypothetical blast scenario in its computer modeling exercise, in which 4kg of RDX was placed on a single column. RDX is the base for a variety of common military explosives, such as C4 and Semtex, and is commonly used in controlled demolitions. They had a few other scenarios in mind, but ruled them out because they "would have required more explosives, or were considered infeasible to accomplish without detection."[60] Their expectations of blast noise were presumably based on RDX, the only explosive they considered. Their rejection of the blast scenario was based on calculations of window breakage from RDX that were not matched by observation of the real event, and by the lack of RDX-level noise being recorded or reported.

In sum, NIST's careful investigation involved not looking for evidence of explosives because it was unlikely to find any, and because the blast sounds weren't likely to be from RDX. NIST's strong sense of likeliness led it to its hypothesis that fire, mainly on one floor, caused a total, symmetrical, free-fall building collapse for the first time in history.

Questions about its approach did persist, however. NIST admirably issued an interim report for public comment. The public commented. The results have been summarized on an FAQ page on the NIST website.[61]

Frequently asked questions included why didn't NIST look at steel samples, and was it possible thermate was used? After FEMA highlighted the biggest mystery of September 11 in the form of vaporized steel and called for further investigation, one might have thought that doing that investigation would be a priority. NIST's response, however, was twofold:

1. Steel? What steel?

2. It wouldn't have mattered anyway.

"Steel samples," claimed NIST, "were removed from the site before the NIST investigation began. In the immediate aftermath of Sept. 11, 2001, debris was removed rapidly from the site to aid in recovery efforts and to facilitate emergency responders' efforts to work around the site. Once it was removed from the scene, the steel from WTC 7 could not be clearly identified."[62]

Besides, said NIST, analyzing the steel for evidence of thermate "would not necessarily have been conclusive" since the chemical byproducts would have been present in the building anyway, e.g., sulfur from gypsum wallboards.[63]

Would it be crazy to say that the NIST approach here is a little disappointing so far? That they've fallen somewhat short of scientific ideals? There are at least three glaring deficiencies in the agency's answers:

1. They said there was no steel when there *was* steel; FEMA had steel. There was a whole special appendix about it. It was covered in *The New York Times*. It was a big mystery.

2. Saying something would not *necessarily* be conclusive leaves open the possibility that it *might* be conclusive, one way or the other. "Why bother when it might fail" isn't the sort of scientific can-do attitude that wins Nobel prizes now is it?

3. This talk of gypsum wallboards is, intentionally or not, a misdirection. It wasn't a question of whether there was sulfur or not, but rather how did sulfur get mixed up in "intergranular melting" in a eutectic reaction? If NIST was insinuating that gypsum wallboards could have somehow accidentally vaporized steel, that is also an idea that could be experimentally demonstrated or refuted.

But let's not obsess over our disappointments. These statements may seem like errors, they may seem to a cynical mind almost like weasel words designed to deceive, but let's not get carried away. We don't want to end up like those paranoid types, wondering if hey, maybe the earth really is flat. Nobody's perfect. Maybe NIST makes up for these shortcomings with its computer model's "probable collapse sequence," which went, as simply as I can render it, as follows:[64]

Heat from fire, primarily in the northeast corner of Floor 12, caused the expansion of five horizontal beams inward from the building's fixed, immobile exterior and pushed a crucial girder off its connections to the columns at either end of it, causing in rapid succession a cascading series of failures that resulted in the demolition-mimicking total building collapse. Floor 13 fell, causing eight floors below it to fall, one at a time, and then columns buckled from east to west, triggering in turn an *upward* progression of floor system failures that reached to the very top of the building.

If you've seen a video of the collapse, you may be thinking hey, hang on. This doesn't sound anything like what it looked like, which was a building dropping all at once, together, not a series of distinct sequential events that could be seen to happen one at a time, however rapidly. This is the very problem NIST had to solve:

When is a unified simultaneous collapse *not* a unified simultaneous collapse?

For the whole building to drop all at once straight down, all 82 inner and outer columns would have to give way in the exact same spots at almost the exact same moment, and that's simply not possible from any amount of fire, never mind scattered fires on a few floors unevenly distributed. We already know it wasn't controlled demolition. That was ruled out. It had to be fire. But how?

Here's the genius bit: The sequence of events described above affected only the entire *inside* of the building, *leaving the exterior shell completely unperturbed*! Twenty-four interior columns and hundreds of beams and girders fell apart so that 47 floor structures ripped free of their connections to 58 external columns without so much as shaking them, and the building crumpled inside like you or I might if we were abandoned by someone who we thought loved us. After that, what we presumed was a whole building falling was really just an empty collapsing exterior façade.

In short, the "probable collapse sequence" is that a girder came loose, the entire inside of the building fell to pieces, and then the outside came down. And that is how a *progressive* collapse came to look just like a simultaneous *global* collapse.

NIST established the likeliness of this hypothesis by using a computer model. There's nothing wrong with using computer models. Indeed, architects and engineers use them all the time. It's how things are done. They're very sophisticated and reliable. Buildings get built using them. We can put a lot of faith in them. They know all about stress and loads and thermal expansion and what happens under various conditions. All the factors are well understood and can be realistically modeled with precision mathematics. These things are amazing.

Still, there are, it seems to me, two main points about the NIST computer model that are troublesome:

1. The animated simulation the model produces looks absolutely nothing like the actual collapse. If you haven't seen it, do go find it. Where the actual observed collapse showed a smooth, symmetrical dropping of a building from the bottom so that it retained its intact shape on the way down – the whole point of the elaborate NIST explanation – the simulation is instead marked by drastic deformations, a warped, contorting exterior that crumples quite asymmetrically, like a can of soda being crushed and twisted by a pair of invisible hands.

2. Even worse, the model's data inputs have been declared secret. Nobody can see them. Why? Because they "might jeopardize public safety."[65] How? They don't say. Maybe there are lots of steel-framed high-rises still standing only because no strategically placed fires on certain floors have caused their entire insides to collapse. What we do know is that the secrecy of the data means that independent peer review is not possible. Obviously, whether or not you accept NIST's rationale for secrecy, this absence of data transparency is a significant deviation from what we'd expect from normal science, whether or not the model proposed a uniquely outlandish and unprecedented occurrence that miraculously mimicked a controlled demolition to perfection.

There's a third thing that is probably worth noting as well, although it's ever so slightly technical. Originally, the NIST report said the collapse-initiating girder was pushed "at least 5.5 inches" off its 11-inch bearing seat. Following the public comment period, it was established that the bearing seat was actually 12 inches wide, to which NIST responded by changing 5.5 inches to 6.25 inches.

Admittedly the new figure remains consistent with "at least 5.5 inches," as would a new figure of 6.25 kilometers, but would it be crazy to think it sounds like these numbers came from human fudging rather than a computer model? The measurement of thermal expansion in a computer model is a function of predictive algorithms processing building materials and construction parameters under this or that fire load. It's not simply taking the width of a bearing seat and saying it had to move at least half of that to fall off. But as a non-expert I don't want to go out on a crazy limb here and have you stop me.

Let's give them the benefit of the doubt and assume their computer model told them those beams would expand at least 5.5 inches, possibly as much as 6.25 inches, but there was mathematical uncertainty for scientific reasons and it couldn't quite pin down an exact figure, and NIST, having very responsibly stated the more conservative estimate, simply changed it to the upper part of the computer-generated range after public objection. That leaves only the confidence-sapping question of how they got the width of the crucial bearing seat wrong in the first place and what that means for their model and its secret inputs but I feel like we're getting bogged down now so let's just drop it.

Perhaps it does sap your confidence though. Perhaps your confidence in NIST's conclusion has also been sapped by its failure to address the mysterious vaporized steel question, its misleading statements about steel availability, its decision not to look for what it doesn't believe it will find, its disregard of recommended fire investigation principles, its narrow assumptions about particular explosives and their noises, its missing the point on sulfur, its debatable positions on likeliness. Perhaps your confidence remains high regardless, perhaps because this is NIST we're talking about, not Joe Schmoe's Goddamned Fudge Factory. It doesn't matter. Let's get one thing straight:

None of these flaws means the NIST theory is incorrect.

It would be great if, in lieu of the peer review we've been denied, some additional properly credentialed experts could take a crack at a computer model of their own, just to see if they could reproduce NIST's findings. Maybe they could, and everything would make sense. If they couldn't, maybe they could tell us why not. Luckily for us and our little intellectual exercise and our critical undogmatic receptiveness, a worthy competing model does in fact exist.

Because of the deficiencies of the NIST report, a small team from the University of Alaska Fairbanks (UAF) led by Dr. Leroy Hulsey, Professor of Structural Engineering, undertook a four-year study to reevaluate the collapse of Building 7. The UAF study had three objectives:

1. To examine the building's structural response to the fire loads of September 11, 2001 (including generating their own simulation as well as examining NIST's hypothesis);

2. To eliminate impossibilities regarding the cause of the observed collapse; and

3. To identify the types and locations of failures that could account for the observed collapse.

The peer-reviewed study concluded that fire did *not* cause the collapse of Building 7. Various analyses all showed that "fires could not have caused weakening or displacement of structural members capable of initiating any of the hypothetical local failures alleged to have triggered the total collapse of the building, nor could any local failures, even if they had occurred, have triggered a sequence of failures that would have resulted in the observed total collapse."[66]

The UAF model tried to make the fire-induced collapse happen with the most generous possible assumptions, but it could not reproduce the NIST findings.

The only way they could get Building 7 to collapse as observed was by the failure of all 82 interior and exterior columns at nearly the same time. Specifically, the study found that "the simultaneous failure of all core columns over 8 stories followed 1.3 seconds later by the simultaneous failure of all exterior columns over 8 stories produces almost exactly the behavior observed in videos of the collapse, whereas no other sequence of failures that we simulated produced the observed behavior."[67]

They did not address the question of what might have *made* 82 interior and exterior columns fail at the same time. They just concluded that this is what had to have happened.

So if they didn't say controlled demolition I'm certainly not going to.

But why should we take *their* word for anything?! Who *are* these guys? Crazy disgruntled fringe characters cooking up bogus models to spread Russian disinformation? Well, Dr. Hulsey appears to have had a long, distinguished, and perfectly respectable career in structural engineering, but that actually isn't what matters. What matters is that his computer model is fully open and transparent, and anyone can download the data, try it in their own software, examine the assumptions and inputs, and see where, if anywhere, his team has fallen prey to Putin's insidious mind-control operations. So far, the model stands, but remains ready for take-down by anybody with a good data-backed argument.

In considering the fire-did-it hypothesis, Hulsey's team used NIST's worst-case temperatures and all of NIST's building construction assumptions. "However," said the UAF report, "it is important to understand that most of these assumptions…are either invalid or at best questionable," such as the exterior columns being "infinitely stiff" when they were actually very flexible. The stiffest bits most resistant to being moved were the inner columns nearest the elevator shaft, so if there were a fixed point from which thermal expansion would extend, it would be from the core pushing outward, not the other way around as NIST had it.[68]

Refer to the UAF report itself for a detailed explanation of what Hulsey's team felt were NIST's erroneous assumptions and missing pieces of building structure. Suffice to say the team was unable to reproduce NIST's results even with assumptions so generous that they definitely departed from earthly reality. Even following NIST's practice of removing all real-life restrictions on lateral movement of beams, such as shear studs, web stiffeners, side plates, and other frames and columns, the UAF model could only get a girder to move a maximum of a mathematically precise-sounding 5.11 inches – short even of NIST's "at least" 5.5, to say nothing of its revised figure of 6.25 inches.

Using actual building construction parameters, it moved less than one inch.

The UAF model also simulated some hypothetical scenarios to see what would happen if the girder *could* drop and the columns *could* fail as a result. They found that:

Columns failing at the lower floors (as per NIST) would not have caused the observed collapse of the east penthouse about 7 seconds before the rest of the collapse; those columns would have had to have failed at an upper floor, well above the fire zone. Forcing the model to fail the implicated columns at lower floors did not collapse the penthouse or cause a horizontal cascade of column failures as NIST predicted. What it did was overload the southeast exterior columns and cause the building to tilt in that direction.

OK. Well what on earth are we hapless lay people to make of all this scientific bickering? Sounds like we can just choose whichever explanation we like better. Whatever gets us through the night, as it were. Do we know who's right and who's wrong? No. Do we know whose model is superior? Not at all. Do we know who's a crazy nut job and who's a con artist and who's a hack and who's a liar? I wish. But no. We do not know.

What *do* we know? We know something about how science is supposed to work. We know it's not supposed to ignore evidence. It's not supposed to draw conclusions that ignore problems like those posed by vaporized steel full of holes with intergranular melting. We know data should be transparent, not declared secret. We know a model should be subject to independent examination.

We know those things, right? It's not crazy to say that we know those things, is it?

Unfortunately, we can't say we know which explanation of the Building 7 collapse is correct. We're not structural engineers. On the bright side, we can say which explanation adheres to our known principles of doing good science and which one — for whatever potentially defensible reason – does not.

So let's go back to the beginning. Here's a highly controversial area in which one's wrong opinion in the absolutist binary can get one tossed into society's Pit of No Return, nut job for life. If you're looking at this little slice of the science of it, at least, and you've got some principles about how science ought to be conducted and some critical undogmatic receptiveness, what do you think? Room for debate? You tell me what's crazy. Should there be a wall of taboo around discussion of this subject, or will that prove to be just – ahem – a collapsing façade?

A Flat Earth

Well I don't know about you but after the previous chapter I need a little break. If I smoked and had a veranda, I'd go outside on the veranda and smoke and, in a contemplative mood, look over the city that I love and ponder the sorry beautiful lot of humanity. We need something lighter now, don't we? Something fun. That was the original idea for this chapter, to lighten the mood, to get our bearings, to take a breath, to have some fun, and what's more fun than laughing at flat earthers? They won't even mind, they're used to it. They're actually very patient with us. Here is the whole chapter, as originally conceived:

It's round, bitches!

That was going to be it! Ha ha ha! A one-line chapter. Finally, an official narrative that stands up to close scrutiny. The earth is round and we're not crazy after all.

But then I thought, as everyone likely thinks after engaging with the flat-earth idea for more than five seconds, well, *why* do these people believe the earth is flat? *How* do they believe it? What are their reasons? How do they explain all the things that are so well explained by the earth being round? They don't have brains the size of a walnut. They're not four feet tall and hairy.

And then I thought, well, maybe a one-line chapter isn't actually enough. Maybe I should go through their main arguments and present a few of the round-earth arguments, and go through the process to do justice to our commitment to critical undogmatic receptiveness and demonstrate that it's not just a pose used to justify nut-job beliefs. Otherwise I'm guilty of what I've been complaining about and failing to subject my own biases to open-minded reevaluation.

And then I thought nah fuck that.

I'm not better than anyone else.

But I was curious enough to watch some flat-earth videos. There was a long one, good couple or three hours, involving two hundred proofs that the earth is flat. I think if anyone has two hundred proofs of anything they must be wrong, and mad to boot. That's an excessive over-abundance of evidence, a sure sign of insanity.

I have to admit I only made it through about eighteen of the proofs. Some of them were interesting. "You expect us to believe that gravity is so strong that it magically holds entire oceans in place on a ball that is spinning rapidly while zooming around the sun, yet it's so weak that a tiny little bird can just up and fly around?"

But my mind was on my chapter. I'd abandoned my one-line idea, but I still wanted it to be short. I wasn't going to go through two hundred of these slippery notions. Plus I had a feeling they'd have two hundred more in the pipeline. I turned off the video.

Then I watched a documentary called *Behind the Curve*,[69] which lets us meet some of the flat earthers while learning about their arguments. It was a disturbing experience. Not because of the flat earthers per se, who, apart from their quirky beliefs and a certain missionary zeal, were (mostly) just nice, normal, seemingly intelligent people with senses of humor.

No, it was mainly disturbing because flat earthers sound like me. They talk about the importance of keeping an open mind and thinking critically. They talk about government corruption and propaganda. They speak in terms of people who are and are not receptive to facts. They implore people to look at evidence. They are convinced that their evidence is so compelling and so logical that it would change people's minds, if only they'd look at it with critical undogmatic receptiveness.

It was disturbing because I told my children about flat earthers and we were laughing and my young daughter said "wow, imagine if your parents were flat earthers" and her face clouded with the imagined shame and even though I agreed with her and agreed with the general perception of flat earthers, I also knew there were things I believed that a lot of people put in the same category as flat earth and all I could think was maybe I better keep quiet about Building 7 before I lose my family.

It was disturbing because there are factions within the flat-earth field — your disc-ers and your infinite-planers, your regular-cosmos-ers and your planetarium-domers — and some flat earthers think other flat earthers are nuts, and it occasionally makes them wonder if they, too, are nuts, but then they reassure themselves that no, they're different, they're the sensible ones, for this or that reason.

It was disturbing because flat earthers can only be in relationships with other flat earthers. That's what they themselves have concluded. There are special dating sites for flat earthers so they can find romance within their belief system. That's not the disturbing part. The disturbing part is that the absolutist binary that keeps flat earthers from getting romantic with round ballers is the same sort of binary that keeps so many other conversations — important ones — from happening.

It was disturbing because perception is reality, facts are puny, and no matter how much evidence I think supports a particular controversial hypothesis, there will always be a lot of people who will look at me like I was looking at those flat earthers, with the same condescending smirk. If your children, your friends, your loved ones decide you're in a category that includes flat earthers, you will find yourself in a very difficult position.

It was disturbing because it featured the obligatory condescending psychologists, whose overly broad and deeply patronizing explanations of the flat-earther mindset implicitly — sometimes explicitly — define the relevant division as the one between official and dissenting narratives rather than the one between well- and poorly supported ones.

It was disturbing because the strong sense of community among flat earthers, apart from being kind of nice, also reveals the part of human nature that finds joy in being an outsider, that is very eager to be in an exclusive club of the few who see the truth, that needs everything to be a secret so they can be let in on it, that is drawn so powerfully to exposé and conspiracy that it can become a form of addiction, with all of addiction's tendency to let rush overrule rationality.

It was disturbing because within that flat-earth community are other human tendencies that overrule rationality or dedication to the truth, like the lure of making a name for yourself within that framework, with the competitiveness that leads also to a focus on heroes and villains instead of principles and exploits a susceptibility to paranoia and plots — a slippery slope indeed.

I've spent a lot of words promoting skeptical questioning. The flat earthers are good at that. But there's a responsibility that comes with that skepticism, which they may not be so good at. It's called being willing to be proven wrong.

In a meandering way we've arrived at last at the point of this chapter. One of the best ways to keep yourself out of the asylum when exercising your skepticism is to have an idea about what would suffice to change your mind about a belief. Is there any kind of evidence that would satisfy you that something wasn't true after all?

Ever heard of a ring laser gyroscope?

A ring laser gyroscope is a very fancy, very accurate, and very expensive machine that detects and measures rotation, e.g., of the earth. Some flat earthers in the documentary bought one. Twenty thousand dollars. They were not just whistling Dixie. They were putting their money where their mouth was. They had, believe it or not, a truly excellent idea for an experiment.

They calculated correctly that for the earth to make a complete rotation of 360 degrees in 24 hours, as claimed by the globe-otomized herd, it must turn 15 degrees per hour (15 times 24 is, erm, let me see, hang on, pencil, ahhhh, yeah, 360). If the earth was really round and really rotating, the ring laser gyroscope would reveal in 60 short minutes that a rotation of 15 degrees had occurred. The flat earthers were quite certain, of course, that it would show no such thing. They were ready to overturn our understanding of the universe using irrefutable science.

They put the fancy widget in its box. They turned it on. They waited.

Perhaps they went out on their verandas. Perhaps they smoked and pondered the sorry beautiful lot of humanity.

After an hour, they took that bad boy out of its box and checked the reading.

Fifteen degrees exactly.

They did it three times with three different kinds of boxes. Three times it said 15 degrees.

They called the results inconclusive.

Twenty thousand bucks.

A Fantastic Vaccine

Vaccine?! Did someone say the word vaccine?! Well he better start saying it's an unmitigated boon to humanity within the next twitch of my left eye or I'm going to run him through with the Anti-Vaxxer Spear and hurl his wretched Neanderthal remains into the Pit of No Return! Only complete idiots speak the word vaccine with anything other than awe and gratitude: That is the overwhelmingly dominant required view. There is nothing more forbidden than being critical of vaccines, their effects, or the system that regulates them. You can ask questions about them, but only if the questions are "where can I get more vaccines?" and "can't we put their critics in jail?"

Relax your shoulders, loosen your face, stop that eye from twitching. Breathe out that anger. Breathe in peace. I'm here to talk about some *positive* vaccine news based, as always here in these pages, on evidence and proper scientific procedures.

The Bandim Health Project (BHP), a research team based in Guinea-Bissau led by Peter Aaby — a Danish anthropologist with a doctoral degree in medicine — published a paper in 1984 that showed a better-than-expected reduction in mortality rates among children who received the measles vaccine in Congo.[70] In other words, mortality rates declined more than could be explained by protection against measles.

This delightful result, which compared outcomes of vaccinated versus unvaccinated populations and was corroborated in several subsequent studies in other countries, demonstrated the existence of vaccine benefits beyond just protection against the target infection. Not only were the vaccinated children better protected than the unvaccinated against measles, their immune systems were evidently strengthened in general such that they showed a lower risk of dying from other infections as well. Aaby is credited with discovering what came to be called "non-specific effects" (NSEs) of vaccines.

Encouraged by its discovery of this excellent vaccine news, and taking note of a gap in the research whereby childhood vaccines had never been studied for their effects on non-target infections, BHP set about investigating all the other childhood vaccines. And guess what?

Wrong! They discovered *more* good news: Every single one of the live vaccines they studied had beneficial NSEs.[71]

And before any haters out there accuse BHP of being funded by Pfizer or Merck or the Bill and Melinda Gates Foundation or any of its vaccine-promoting minion organizations, it's not so. They receive some core funding from the University of Southern Denmark, and then grants for individual projects from governmental and private foundations that play no role in directing the research. They declare themselves independent and free from conflicts of interest. They are not paid shills for Big Pharma. They're researchers. Researchers who care about the children of Guinea-Bissau.

But they did also discover that several non-live vaccines had *harmful* NSEs.

Data for a non-live vaccine called DTP (for Diphtheria, Tetanus, and Pertussis) — which BHP had introduced in Guinea-Bissau, believing it to be beneficial — showed that very young DTP-vaccinated children had five times *higher* mortality than their DTP-unvaccinated counterparts overall; for vaccinated girls that rate was *ten* times higher.[72] They were well protected from the three target infections – the vaccine did what it said it would do – but evidently at the cost of a greatly weakened general immune system. They died as a result of greater susceptibility to a range of other infections.

It's also important to note that the deleterious effects appeared to be mitigated, although not eliminated, by receipt of measles or BCG vaccine with or after the DTP vaccination. So, there are multiple factors. It's not absolutely binary: vaccine good or vaccine bad. There's a whole complex picture begging for discussion and investigation. Without name calling or banishment from society.

When BHP took its alarming safety signal to the World Health Organization (WHO), the WHO commissioned seven other studies to test the BHP findings. None replicated the observation of increased child mortality rates, but all had the same methodological flaw that introduced bias: they based their data on periodic visits, with vaccination status updated on the second visit. Children who were unvaccinated as of the first visit, then got vaccinated, then died before the second visit were still counted as unvaccinated. The WHO later acknowledged the bias and said they'd "keep a watch" on NSEs.[73]

The WHO also proceeded to analyze ten other DTP studies and finally confirmed the negative NSEs, and confirmed that the negative effect was more pronounced for girls. BHP also did additional studies for children in different age groups and published a combined analysis of three studies in 2018. It showed that "the introduction of DTP vaccine in Guinea-Bissau was associated with a 2-fold increase in overall mortality" (2.6-fold for girls) in children between 6 and 35 months.[74]

A 2020 BHP analysis of all the DTP studies (17 in all) again showed a slightly more than doubled rate of vaccinated versus unvaccinated all-cause mortality overall, with girls dying at a rate of about 50 percent more than boys.[75] Furthermore, a dose-response relationship was observed, i.e., more doses of DTP equated to higher all-cause mortality rates.

BHP also found that DTP is not the only non-live vaccine that is associated with increased female mortality. The same negative NSEs that were found for DTP were also found for the malaria vaccine, the inactivated polio vaccine, the hepatitis B vaccine, the pentavalent vaccine (DTP plus Hep B and Haemophilus influenzae type b), and the H1N1 flu vaccine. These are all non-live vaccines. As BHP researcher Christine Benn notes: "No bias can explain why only non-live vaccines should be negative for females."[76]

Just in case you thought BHP researchers' minds had been poisoned by an anti-vaxxing team of Russian disinformation specialists, it is also noteworthy that they do not call for banning vaccines with negative NSEs. The organization instead maintains that it should be possible to design vaccination programs that combine non-live and mitigating live vaccines in a way that keeps children safe.

Did the right science things happen here? Studies revealed alarming safety signals, they were reported up the chain. There was a bit of pushback but ultimately other studies corroborated the result. Nobody was banned, demonetized, marginalized, fired. Useful new knowledge was obtained, including the following points:

- Not all vaccines are the same.

- Studies of vaccinated versus unvaccinated populations are important and can reveal unexpected effects, both good and bad. We should probably do more of them.

- It's important to study *all-cause* mortality and morbidity – overall health outcomes – and not just focus on the target infections.

- If we discover bad news, we can come up with ideas for solutions.

Should it be possible in a normal democratic society that values public health, science, truth, and civil liberties to talk about potential vaccine harms like we talk about most anything else, without everyone losing their minds and reflexively hurling thought-crushing pejoratives like anti-vaxxer?

What do you think? Is that crazy to say? Are we all still here?

Given the fact that nobody actually denies that serious adverse events do occur – add the obligatory disclaimer rarely here if you like – and that some vaccines have turned out to be harmful enough to be pulled from the market — I'm sorry but it's true, it has occurred, here on earth, in reality, I didn't make it up[77] — shouldn't there be *some* room in society, *some*where, for people to voice a concern without everyone getting hysterical?

Let's be serene. Let's smile and breathe and think it through calmly. The most extreme possible form of vaccine advocacy would have to be that 100 percent of vaccines are 100 percent safe and 100 percent effective for 100 percent of the population. If you believed that only 99.9 percent of vaccines were 100 percent safe and 100 percent effective for 100 percent of the population, should you be called an anti-vaxxer and cast into the Pit for deviating slightly from the most total possible form of vaccine advocacy?

I think not. I think you should be given a chance to explain your right-wing anti-science moronic heresy to a jury of critical undogmatic receivers.

So at what point must someone be tagged with the dreaded absolutist discussion-ending pejorative? If one of their percentages deviates an arbitrarily determined amount from the extreme? If they identify a single exception to the total advocacy general rule? Two exceptions? Three?

If they want to read more about one of them?

If they accept the Institute of Medicine's conclusion that the existing vaccine adverse events reporting system (VAERS) captures only one percent of adverse events?[78]

If they think it's a conflict of interest for regulators to share in profits and patent rights, or to go through the revolving door into high-paid pharmaceutical industry jobs?

If they think it would be a good idea to do more comparative studies of vaccinated versus unvaccinated populations?

If they want to ask about risk-benefit analyses for different groups?

If they know that correlation doesn't prove causation, but they think strong correlations warrant thorough investigation?

If they're worried about a reaction their child had?

If they think that a vaccine with over 22,000 death reports in VAERS in three years should be looked at quite carefully even though the reports prove nothing about causality?

Should these kinds of concerns yield dispassionate, nuanced, science-based discussions among people with a shared interest in determining the truth, or should they trigger shrill reflexive bouts of name-calling?

Imagine if nobody had listened to BHP's alarming safety signals. Imagine if the responsible scientists were called nut jobs and hounded out of their jobs. Wouldn't that be crazy bad dystopian wrong?

In the unlikely event there was a vaccine rollout that was temporally and demographically correlated with a persistent significant increase in excess deaths, cardiovascular problems, strokes, weird long rubbery white blood clots, and unusual aggressive cancers across all age groups, we'd surely expect that the necessary studies would be kicked into high gear pronto without anyone being called a stupid lunatic for noticing the problem. All reasonable hypotheses would be welcomed in the search for answers that public health science would demand.

That's how we'd know we were living in a normal democratic pro-science society and not one suffering from a corrupt system of greedy mega-corporations and captured regulators.

A DANGEROUS MEDICINE

You are not a horse. You are not a cow. Seriously y'all. Stop it.
                                        –FDA, via Twitter[79]

In the middle of the Covid pandemic, as you may recall, certain apparently insane doctors tried to give horse dewormer to their patients in what must have been a deranged attempt to kill them off. What can they have been thinking? Perhaps they were eugenicists, convinced that the real problem was overpopulation. Either that or they were surrealists, convinced that their patients were horses.

When it wasn't mad doctors, it was "conservative commentators" and "fringe groups" and "vaccine skeptics" who were responsible for "hyping the horse paste." Evidently, whatever this chemical compound was, it had political leanings. It probably leaked out of Donald Trump's secret bioweapons horse ranch laboratory. His alt-right minions went nuts for equine edibles and began ingesting the substance with wild abandon, probably washing it down with household bleach, with disastrous consequences. I mean if there was brain damage, who'd even be able to tell?

The compound in question is of course ivermectin. Even though this is obviously an open-and-shut case of morons abusing a veterinary medicine based on outrageously bad information from the world's worst doctors conspiring with right-wing nut jobs, we shall perform our due diligence and give the case the critical undogmatic receptiveness treatment. It would take an entire book to tell this story properly, and fortunately there is one.[80] Well worth reading. For our own part, we'll make do with a brief summary to get the basic lay of the land.

As always, we're not going to try to settle any medical questions or pretend to be subject experts. We'll stick to our focus on whether normal procedures of science and democracy occurred, or whether something else happened. We will, however, need to take a peek at the science just to establish that there is some. So what do we know about this so-called medicine?

Ivermectin was isolated in the 1970s by Satoshi Omura, head of the Antibiotics Research Group at the Kitasato Institute in Tokyo, from a single microorganism found only in Japanese soil. Originally tested as a veterinary drug, it was soon found to be highly effective against a number of major parasitic diseases that afflict humans. Today it is used as a "wonder drug" against river blindness, elephantiasis, and a range of other tropical diseases plaguing the human beings of the developing world.

In addition to its anti-parasitic effects, which were its initial claim to fame, ivermectin has been found to possess potent anti-viral and anti-inflammatory properties and "new uses for it are continually being found."[81]

Ivermectin has proven to be such an important and versatile drug that in 2015 its discoverers won the Nobel Prize in medicine. Statues have been erected in its honor outside the World Bank and the World Health Organization (WHO) for its contribution to eliminating river blindness. It is on the WHO list of essential medicines and is considered, along with penicillin and aspirin, to be among a small handful of drugs that have had the greatest impact on world health.

It is also an "astonishingly safe"[82] drug: With more than 4 billion doses having been administered to humans over several decades, only 28 serious neurological adverse events have occurred, according to the *American Journal of Therapeutics*,[83] making it far safer than common over-the-counter drugs like acetaminophen (Tylenol or Paracetamol), which is the second-most common cause of liver failure worldwide and is responsible for 500 deaths and 56,000 emergency room visits per year in the United States.[84]

Even better, ivermectin is an off-patent generic medicine costing only pennies per dose.

That's all fine and dandy, but let's get one thing straight: ivermectin is not FDA-approved for Covid treatment! OK? You got that?

It *is* FDA-approved as safe and effective for other diseases, but any use of ivermectin against Covid would constitute what they call an off-label usage.

Let's get one other thing straight: there is nothing more ordinary in medicine than off-label prescriptions. Don't take my word for it. Ask your doctor. Or listen to the National Cancer Institute, which states that "once the FDA approves a drug, doctors can prescribe it for any purpose they think makes sense for the patient."[85] Happens all the time. Basic medical practice. Not controversial. That's why we have doctors who do all that education. Ivermectin, for example, is very commonly used for scabies. It is not FDA-approved for scabies. Nobody makes a fuss. Why? Because it works, it's safe, and that's what doctors do. They prescribe legal medicines they think will safely work.

Dr. Pierre Kory and Dr. Paul Marik are two of the most notable proponents of ivermectin against Covid. Dr. Kory is an experienced pulmonary and critical care expert who, at the time of the pandemic, was in charge of the intensive care unit (ICU) at University of Wisconsin Hospital and Chief of the Medical Critical Care Service. Dr. Marik is the most published practicing critical care specialist in the history of the discipline, with over 500 peer-reviewed journal articles to his credit, along with 80 book chapters and four books on critical care. He's been cited more than 43,000 times in peer-reviewed publications. He is known, among other things, for revolutionary, paradigm-shifting work in sepsis care and the resuscitation of people in shock from dangerously low blood pressure.

An h-index is a measure of a doctor or scientist's impact on their field. A professor will typically have an h-index of 12 to 24, while a Nobel Prize winner will often have one above 30. Dr. Marik's h-index is 110.

So, just to be clear: we're not talking about horse doctors here.

Ivermectin wasn't the first thing they tried. Under the pressure of the rolling pandemic emergency, they networked with leading specialists around the world, working nonstop, reading and sharing observations, findings, and insights from direct clinical experience as well as hundreds of emerging papers and preprint manuscripts.

This group, which became known as the Front Line Covid Critical Care Alliance (FLCCC),[86] developed and disseminated a treatment protocol involving corticosteroids, high-dose intravenous vitamin C, thiamine, and other interventions. They halved the mortality rate other ICUs were experiencing. It was excellent news: Covid was serious, but it was a treatable disease using potent, multi-mechanistic, existing therapies. Their pioneering work directly led to corticosteroids becoming the worldwide standard of care for hospitalized Covid patients, overturning NIH and WHO guidelines that had previously recommended against it.[87]

The FLCCC doctors, incidentally, were almost all liberal Democrats. Not that politics matters in medicine.

During an FLCCC Zoom call in October of 2020, Dr. Marik shared the news that ivermectin was showing promise against Covid according to a handful of preprint papers and one peer-reviewed article in a high-ranking medical journal. It was only one study but it seemed sound and showed a 47 percent reduction in mortality among all treated patients, and a 73 percent reduction among the most seriously ill.[88]

Intrigued, Dr. Kory looked into the existing literature and found over a dozen in vitro studies since 2012 showing that ivermectin stopped replication of at least ten different viruses, including Zika, West Nile, HIV, and influenza.[89] Most of them were RNA viruses, as was SARS-CoV2. It was clear that ivermectin was not just a broad-spectrum anti-parasitic but also a broad-spectrum anti-viral agent. But that was in vitro. Test tubes. What about in real life?

Dr. Kory's next discovery was a mass ivermectin distribution program in Peru called Operation Tayta. In every region where ivermectin was deployed, Covid cases rapidly declined, in contrast to the one place it was not deployed, Lima, where cases and deaths continued to rise. When the program was discontinued by Peru's newly elected president, cases and deaths skyrocketed in those locations once again.[90]

It turned out that everywhere ivermectin distribution programs were tried — Argentina, Brazil, Dominican Republic, India, Mexico, Paraguay, Peru, the Philippines — they resulted in massive reductions in hospitalizations and deaths.

In Mexico City, an ivermectin distribution program resulted in a significant reduction in hospitalization of between 52 and 76 percent in a test population of nearly 80,000 patients.[91]

Between March and November 2020, 2,706 patients with Covid symptoms at a hospital in the Dominican Republic were given ivermectin in the emergency room and sent home. Only sixteen returned and needed hospitalization. Of those, two died. That's 2,704 survivors out of 2,706 people sick enough to go to the emergency room, and 2,690 who didn't require hospitalization.[92]

Another early clue: As a result of a scabies outbreak at a nursing home in France in mid 2020, all the residents and staff members were given ivermectin. Then the first surge of Covid hit the region. Only 1.4 percent of the people got infected; nobody needed oxygen, was hospitalized, or died. The other nursing homes in the same region had an infection rate of 22.6 percent, with nearly 5 percent of the people dying. The doctors at the scabies nursing home published a paper attributing their good fortune to the serendipitous application of ivermectin.[93]

The big one was the state of Uttar Pradesh in India, with a population of 230 million in an area the size of the United Kingdom. Covid's Delta wave initially hit Uttar Pradesh hard, with millions of migrant workers bringing the variant into the state. As the Delta wave cases began to rise, the Chief Minister rolled out a Rapid Response Team of 400,000 healthcare workers to 97,000 villages to perform testing and provide ivermectin to patients and close contacts alike. According to a Johns Hopkins University study, over 33,000 cases in Uttar Pradesh in late April 2020 had dropped to 18,000 by May 12. By the end of May, a state of 230 million people, massively testing, was seeing fewer than 600 new cases per day; by the summer's end, Covid had almost completely disappeared from Uttar Pradesh. The *Hindustan Times* reported in early September that 67 of Uttar Pradesh's 75 districts had reported no new cases in the previous 24 hours. During the same time period, 226,000 tests had been administered, resulting in eleven positives. In 33 districts there were zero active cases. In the entire state, there were 199 active cases. This was at the height of the pandemic. Across the rest of India, Delta continued to rage.[94]

In addition to the encouraging real-world clinical experience, there have been numerous studies of ivermectin's efficacy on various outcomes. As of this writing there have been 103 studies comparing treatment and control groups, including 50 double-blind randomized control trials (RCTs), involving 1,193 scientists and 142,417 patients in 29 countries, overwhelmingly showing statistically significant improvement in mortality, ventilation, ICU, hospitalization, time to recovery, viral clearance, and prophylaxis.[95]

Tess Lawrie is an expert reviewer of medical evidence who has published numerous reviews in top medical journals and databases, including the prestigious Cochrane Library, and contributed to treatment guidelines used by the WHO and the UK's National Health Service. She was initially skeptical of the FLCCC news about ivermectin. Evidence synthesis being one of her fields of expertise, she performed a meta-analysis of the existing ivermectin studies and concluded:

> This review and meta-analysis confirms that ivermectin substantially reduces the risk of a person dying from COVID-19 by probably somewhere in the region of 65% to 92% according to RCT data. The uncertainty in the evidence relates to the precise extent of the reduction, not in the effectiveness of ivermectin itself. Similarly, when ivermectin is used as prophylaxis among health care workers and contacts, it is clear that ivermectin substantially reduces COVID-19 infections, probably somewhere in the region of 88% (82% to 92%)…Not only is ivermectin a safe, effective and well-known medicine, at an estimated cost of less than 10 pence per person treated with a 12 mg tablet, it does indeed seem like a miracle drug in the context of the current global COVID-19 situation.[96]

Other meta-analyses followed. A meta-analysis of 42 clinical studies, including 21 RCTs, in the *Japanese Journal of Antibiotics*, showed 83 percent improvement in early treatment, 51 percent in late treatment, and 89 percent in preventing the disease in the first place. First author Morimasa Yagisawa concluded that, from a statistical perspective, the probability that ivermectin was *not* effective against Covid was one in four trillion.[97]

Considering also its stellar safety profile, you might think this hopeful news — potentially a way to stop the pandemic in its tracks — would have resulted in the WHO, the NIH, the NHS, every national government, and the mainstream media rushing to promote ivermectin as, at the very least, one powerful (and inexpensive) weapon in the anti-Covid arsenal.

You'd be as wrong as it is possible to be.

In fact, if you checked the news then, it would be much the same as if you googled it right now. You'd mainly see two things: articles about the *lack* of evidence favoring this "unproven" drug ivermectin that was not FDA-approved for Covid, and articles about how a bunch of right-wing yahoos are promoting horse paste because they're so stupid.

What's going on here? No matter how misleading the veterinary angle clearly is, there still must be some tangible reason for this anti-ivermectin vehemence. And yes. There were essentially three things:

1. a case of apparent fraud in one positive ivermectin study;

2. reports of ivermectin-related injuries; and

3. six studies published in high-impact journals that found that there was insufficient evidence to say that ivermectin was useful in treating or preventing Covid.

Each of these instances was followed immediately by major headlines in the news saying ivermectin doesn't work, and much gleeful mockery on social media of the demented doctors and right-wing imbeciles and their horse paste follies.

The absolutist binary strikes again. If you weren't properly scornful of ivermectin, your pathetic pleas for dispassionate science would fade with you into the Pit of No Return.

The case of apparent fraud involved a paper by Ahmed Elgazzar *et al*, which was withdrawn over disputed validity of source data.[98] Several meta-analyses had to be recalculated as a result of this paper's retraction, with the overall results still favoring ivermectin. The real problem was that news reports made it sound like *all* the pro-ivermectin studies were tarred with the brush of fraud, even though it was a single study out of almost a hundred. For mainstream news outlets, it didn't matter if there were fifty or a hundred or two hundred or five million positive ivermectin studies — positive ivermectin studies were now fraudulent. Full stop.

The case of ivermectin injuries in the news is a sordid tale, which I will tell as briefly as possible. Shortly after the FDA issued its infamous "You are not a horse" tweet (which it was later forced by a lawsuit to take down), the CDC issued a health advisory that went to every state health department and licensed doctor in the United States. The memo noted the rapid increase in ivermectin prescriptions and warned of reports of severe illnesses associated with "products containing ivermectin."

It turns out the sole basis for this health advisory was six telephone calls to the Mississippi health department, four of which pertained to the veterinary version. Mild symptoms of uncertain origin were reported. No overdoses. No deaths. No ambulances. No hospitalizations. Yet the nation's doctors were put on high alert about the newfound dangers of prescribing ivermectin.

This narrative was given a boost when *Rolling Stone* printed an entirely false story about gunshot victims in Oklahoma left waiting because horse dewormer overdoses had "overwhelmed" hospitals. By the time *Rolling Stone* admitted the story was fake and quietly retracted it, the American Medical Association and two pharmaceutical associations had called for "an immediate end to prescribing, dispensing, or using ivermectin to prevent or treat Covid." Once-proud, Nobel Prize-winning, WHO-listed essential medicine ivermectin had been reduced to a national joke.[99]

If all we wanted to do was dismiss ivermectin and the right-wing lunatics we believed were its main advocates, we'd be done. We'd have fraud and overwhelmed hospitals and morons from Oklahoma and all the scientific data we needed. Big studies in reputable journals said it didn't work. Case closed. These were in the major media, so we know they're respectable studies. Those other studies, the positive ones, if we even know they exist, well, we don't have to think about them anymore. They must be from crackpot sheep-shaggers in MAGA hats doing so-called studies between shots of moonshine out by the makeshift still.

Except, lest we forget, we do know that some of the doctors behind those studies are among the top critical care experts in the world, so... if we're still really determined to hate ivermectin with the kind of single-minded vehemence we like to have, we could always just dismiss all those positive studies by, well, perhaps by waving our hands dismissively.

Cognitive dissonance can be ignored for a surprisingly long time. Maybe forever.

But maybe, if we honestly wanted to get to the bottom of this thing, we might have some reasonable questions about what makes 97 of 103 studies wrong, unreliable, and not worth talking about, and the other six definitive and worthy of dominating not just the headlines but the whole official medical narrative.

We of course as lay people are not in a very good position to compare the studies, or, say, the *types* of studies. But are there any differences between these six studies — and we can add a seventh, Oxford's PRINCIPLE trial, although it was not published in a high-impact journal — and all the other ones that were so strongly positive? Any differences that we, even as humble lay people of average intelligence, might have some hope of grasping?

Turns out there are a few things about the methodologies that are noteworthy and comprehensible. Perhaps the most important thing is that, unlike the positive studies, which emphasized the importance of early treatment within two or three days of symptoms, these seven negative studies were late-treatment studies, allowing up to fourteen days before treatment. Also, the dosages were lower than those recommended in the positive studies, and of shorter duration. One of the FLCCC protocols was to ensure ivermectin was taken with food, leading to absorption of higher concentrations of medicine; the negative studies recommended ivermectin on an empty stomach for some reason.

One of the studies had an original primary endpoint of time to clinical recovery at fourteen days. The study showed statistically significant benefit of ivermectin at seven days, and again at fourteen days. Good news for ivermectin. But then, mid-study, they decided to double the endpoint to twenty-eight days, by which time the statistical significance had disappeared.

Changing a trial's endpoint midway through is normally considered a sign of scientific fraud and misconduct.[100] In this case, nobody minded.,

Another factor was that most of the studies were conducted in South America where ivermectin was available over the counter and in wide general use. *Nature* magazine reported on the problem of establishing and maintaining a viable control group of non-ivermectin users under these conditions.[101] In one trial, the placebo group was actually given ivermectin for a while as the result of a mislabeling incident. As Dr. Kory has noted, it is very hard to prove that ivermectin is more effective than ivermectin.

Another issue was that most of the studies enrolled only mildly ill, young, and healthy people. Hospitalization was so low throughout these studies that they were what is called "under-powered," i.e., unable to generate statistical significance.

Finally, it may also be noteworthy that these negative studies, unlike their positive counterparts, were funded by sources with an interest in promoting new patented drugs in direct competition with cheap generic ivermectin.[102]

But again, what are we, doctors? Scientists? No! We don't know whether these negative studies that happened to be music to Big Pharma's ears were designed to fail on purpose or whether that contentious suggestion is just the sort of thing you'd expect from a bunch of losers who can't stand to see their flimsy horse research kicked to the curb by superior science.

If the negative studies were not intentionally designed to sabotage ivermectin, however, with low doses, short treatments, late starts, and underpowered cohorts, it would be difficult to argue that they were designed to give the drug its best chance.

The thing is, as hard as they may have tried to minimize the drug's advantages, they still, all of them, showed ivermectin to be better at most outcomes than the placebo — sometimes even in a statistically significant manner. The strange result is reports with data showing that people did better with ivermectin, and conclusions saying the evidence isn't strong enough.[103]

That's a lot of don't-even-try-it for a might-help drug that's way safer than Tylenol.

One other way we, even as lay people, can get a sense of what's going on with these headline-generating negative trials is to compare them with trials for Covid treatments that *succeeded* in getting the coveted WHO and FDA recommendations. This is particularly easy to do in the case of the antiviral molnupiravir because it had the same principal investigator, Chris Butler, as the Oxford/PRINCIPLE ivermectin trial.

In Butler's ivermectin trial ("the most clearly designed-to-fail trial, with major bias in design, operation, analysis, and reporting"[104]), treatment could be delayed as much as 14 days — "a delay incompatible with the use of antiviral treatments, and incompatible with current real-world protocols"[105]; in his molnupiravir trial, the limit was 5 days, with a median of 2. His ivermectin trial was open to anyone 18 or over; his molnupiravir trial was open to those 50 or over, or younger if they had comorbidities. The ivermectin treatment protocol was once a day for three days — "no other antiviral is ever used for less than five days"[106] — at a low dosage below the real-world recommendation; the molnupiravir protocol called for two doses per day for five days. The ivermectin trial specified administration without food, against real-world recommendations; for molnupiravir, the recommendation was with or without food. The cost for molnupiravir treatment was over $700; for ivermectin, less than a dollar.

Despite the differences and built-in biases of methodologies, ivermectin outperformed molnupiravir, but it was molnupiravir — which, incidentally, was first developed to treat encephalitis…in horses,[107] no I'm not kidding — that received FDA Emergency Use Authorization in December 2021[108] and got added to the WHO's Covid treatment guidelines in March of 2022.[109]

Post-marketing studies of FDA's adverse events reports were conducted because of "the weakness of the current evidence supporting [molnupiravir's] widespread use."[110] Researchers found "an unexpectedly high rate of serious adverse reactions" including seizure, renal impairment, arrhythmia, cardiac arrest, and cardiac failure.[111] Seventy deaths were reported as resulting from molnupiravir. In November of 2023, the WHO withdrew its recommendation for molnupiravir, "judging the potential harms to outweigh the limited benefits."[112]

By then, Merck had already made over $7 billion on sales of molnupiravir.[113]

Remdesivir, the first antiviral to be approved for use against Covid, was found by most trials to have no clinical benefits whatsoever.[114] Indeed one large study found it was associated with *longer* hospital stays.[115] Even worse, it's associated with a "disproportionately high number of kidney and liver problems"[116] — to the point that nurses began referring to the drug as RunDeathIsNear.[117] It was originally tested as an Ebola drug, but was withdrawn from that trial because of its lethal side effects, including multiple organ failure, acute kidney failure, and septic shock, afflicting more than 30 percent of its recipients. Its mortality rate was the highest among the four drugs trialed.[118]

That seems worth repeating: remdesivir was deemed *too dangerous to be used to treat Ebola*, a disease with a 50 percent mortality rate.

Despite that failure and the fact that it was not FDA approved for any purpose, it was granted Emergency Use Authorization and became the standard of care for hospitalized Covid patients.[119] The WHO initially recommended against use of remdesivir for Covid "regardless of how severely ill they are" because the drug "has no meaningful effect on mortality or on other important outcomes for patients,"[120] but eventually made a conditional recommendation for its use in patients with severe Covid.[121] At over $3,000 per treatment, Gilead pulled in just over $15 billion in revenue for remdesivir between 2020 and the first quarter of 2024.[122]

So, scientifically, where does that leave us? On the one hand we've got ivermectin, long considered one of the safest drugs in the world with over four billion doses having been administered to humans for various diseases over the years and almost no safety issues having been raised. Nobel Prize. Statues. There were seven studies with negative conclusions despite their own data favoring ivermectin on most outcomes, and almost a hundred studies showing dramatic, possibly pandemic-ending benefits for both treatment and prevention at pennies per dose. The relevant authorities not only didn't recommend it, they issued stern warnings against using it.

Doctors have had their licenses come under attack for prescribing it; pharmacies have refused to fill valid prescriptions; people have been kicked off social media platforms for speaking positively of it. Peer-reviewed papers have been retracted and rejected without errors being identified, without opportunities for revision. Completely false news stories have been printed about nonexistent poisonings.

On the other hand, we've got drugs with horrendous safety profiles like molnupiravir and remdesivir, with deeply unimpressive studies, getting glowing press coverage and fast-track Emergency Use Authorizations, whereupon they generate multi-billion-dollar profits, at least until they're pulled from the market for harms outweighing benefits.

Would it be crazy to say that ivermectin is being held to a radically different standard than its competitors?

Why would that be the case?

Let's not be party to any irresponsible speculation about malign influence. What we need here is some sober perspective from distinguished insider experts who aren't as inclined towards conspiracy theories as some of the rest of us:

> *Journals have devolved into information-laundering operations for the pharmaceutical industry.*[123]
> – Richard Horton, former editor of *The Lancet*

> *Now primarily a marketing machine to sell drugs of dubious benefit, this industry uses its wealth and power to co-opt every institution that might stand in its way, including the U.S. Congress, the Food and Drug*

Administration, academic medical centers, and the medical profession itself... [D]uring my two decades at The New England Journal of Medicine.... I saw companies begin to exert a level of control over the way research is done that was unheard of when I first came to the journal, and the aim was clearly to load the dice to make sure their drugs looked good ... I became increasingly troubled by the possibility that much published research is seriously flawed, leading doctors to believe new drugs are generally more effective and safer than they actually are.[124]

– Marcia Angell, former editor of *The New England Journal of Medicine*

The medical profession is being bought by the pharmaceutical industry, not only in terms of the practice of medicine, but also in terms of teaching and research. The academic institutions of this country are allowing themselves to be the paid agents of the pharmaceutical industry. I think it's disgraceful.[125]

– Arnold Relman, another former editor of *The New England Journal of Medicine*

We have now reached a point where those doing systematic reviews must start by assuming that a study is fraudulent until they can have some evidence to the contrary.[126]

– Richard Smith, former editor of *The British Medical Journal*

All three of the principal [US] health agencies suffer from agency capture. A large portion of the FDA's budget is provided by pharmaceutical companies. NIH is cozy with biomedical and pharmaceutical companies and its scientists are allowed to collect royalties on drugs NIH licenses to pharma. And as the former director of the Centers for Disease Control and Prevention (CDC), I know the agency can be influenced by special interest groups.[127]

– Robert Redfield, former CDC Director

Pharmaceutical companies corupting research, information, education, and regulation? Would it be crazy to suggest that, in an ideal world, startling observations like these from the highest-level insiders would be bigger news? Alarms would be sounded? We wouldn't just shrug it off? Things would change? At the very least, we'd absorb the information and apply the knowledge to our understanding of what we see happening?

It's not as if the interests of the pharmaceutical industry are synonymous with the interests of public health. On the contrary, there is a rich history of flagrant industry disregard for public health, full of episodes like Merck's cynical manipulation of its Vioxx data, which "led to thousands of avoidable premature deaths and 100,000 heart attacks"[128] before it was finally pulled from the market.

Since 2000, the total amount of financial penalties against the pharmaceutical industry for a variety of profit-driven ethical lapses is, at the time of this writing ... any guesses?

$116,245,163,450.[129]

That's $116.2 billion. Buh buh buh buh billion.

These are obviously not victimless crimes. Indeed it's difficult not to conclude we're talking about an industry with a rather cavalier attitude to the health consequences of its products and an inordinate amount of social influence. When $116 billion is an acceptable write-off, maybe there's enough money being made to skew a few priorities.

What shall we make of all this? Is this important context? Does it mean anything? Do you think ivermectin got a fair shake? Are science and democracy working properly here? Is it just possible that something else is going on here? Your call.

CONCLUSION

The earth is round and we should talk more. Those are my conclusions. I'm leaving any other conclusions to you, as promised. The aspiration of this book has been to chip away at some artificial barriers to communication, not to change your mind about which positions in our case studies you feel are ultimately correct. By way of wrapping up, I will offer a few thoughts about what I believe has been demonstrated. I may even wax slightly philosophical, but hopefully not to the point where you have to slap me.

In our small handful of controversial case studies, we've looked at a few non-trivial issues that typically receive the absolutist binary treatment: there's an official sane view for sensible people and there's ridiculous nonsense from lunatics and morons. There's nothing in between except an impenetrable wall. For sensible people even to peek over that wall is to risk not only social opprobrium but falling into the unnerving abyss of a potentially bottomless rabbit hole. So people tend not to. Understandably.

However, avoiding those discomforts necessarily entails another risk: that of accepting false narratives and the authoritarian mechanisms that protect them, which could ultimately have consequences even greater than friends and family rolling their eyes at you behind your back. Caught between two kinds of unpleasantness in a space of uncertain truth suggests that a bit of critical undogmatic receptiveness might be in order, so as to make more informed choices and end up, so to speak, on the right side of history. One cannot be neutral on a moving train, as the late great historian Howard Zinn has observed.[130]

Our case studies have shown, I think, that there is a jarring disconnect between the quality of the tabooed arguments and what we might call their social standing. With one instructive exception that shows we can tell the difference between controversy and quackery (sorry, flat earthers), it is clear that these arguments – right or wrong – are working within the bounds of science and, at the very least, are not the evidence-free crackpot ravings they are so often purported to be. In a world where science and democracy actually mattered, not only would they be eminently deserving of a fair hearing, society would welcome the debate. Society would *demand* the debate.

That being the case, one wonders how and why these dissenting views have been tabooed.

Generally speaking, the "why" of tabooing (as opposed to countering) an idea is to discourage people from even considering it. In the context of science, it's difficult to think of a plausible motivation other than to protect hypotheses that are not robust enough to survive disinterested competition – to disguise preferred narratives as unassailable truths – and of course ultimately to protect the beneficiaries of those narratives.

The "how" is perhaps the more vexing question, and one that goes beyond the scope of the present work. There are plenty of books and articles about the workings of propaganda and the burgeoning censorship industrial complex. What we can say briefly here is that the tabooing of legitimate dissent is an indictment of the norm-shaping institutions of society, and an affront to the principles upon which democracy and science depend. Implicated in particular is a failure of journalism, which is meant to be probing and adversarial, not obsequious and promotional.

Also implicated are we the people. Hence our other concern here has been to demonstrate that we don't necessarily have to be highly trained subject experts to get an idea about what's going on with an issue. There are ways, fully within our grasp, to tell flat-earth silliness from a controversial idea that has some merit. We're not helpless. We don't have to swallow everything we're fed. Our brains work. We know how to think, once we realize there's something to think about. We have a responsibility to each other to do so. It is our only defense against propaganda. It is the only way democracy can fulfill its promise.

The whole disinformation obsession of our times is based on the paternalistic view that people are too stupid to evaluate information on their own. Which is only slightly less insulting than the companion notion that what is needed isn't critical thinking but a set of approved sources. The fact that we live in a world where "malinformation"– information that is somehow disreputable despite being true – is a word that gets used with a straight face should give us all a permanent skeptical squint.

If we accept that much, it suggests that our responsibility to think means we don't go on mental autopilot the moment we hear one of the mindless pejoratives that comprise the essential staples of the "how" of tabooing. It means we don't just nod our heads when we're told that a medicine is right wing, or that authoritarianism is left wing, or that a lab leak is a conspiracy theory, or that anyone who thinks correlations should be investigated is an anti-vaxxer.

These pejorative terms, intended to end conversations, should rather start them. Or so it seems to me.

We have looked at issues that have a scientific basis, not because science issues are the most important and not because we hope to understand the evidence (although sometimes we can), but because they can be tested: We know the *conduct* of the science must adhere to certain well-known standards. If we can find clear breaches of those standards, then we have something more tangible to grasp than the contested murk of opinions, values, and ideological preferences. Scientific misconduct gives us a firm basis for evaluating the legitimacy of norms and taboos.

A position that rests on weak science is weak, no matter how widely accepted it may be. If a widely accepted belief is both false and unquestionable, we have a societal delusion. If it gets bad enough, we have a world gone mad.

That's the other reason we choose to look at issues with a scientific basis. If the world has gone mad, then just describing it accurately will make you sound – and feel – like a nutjob. Staying tethered to science is exceptionally useful as a sanity check.

Let's not be coy about where all this leaves us: Once again with the telling exception of round earth science – and I do feel bad piling onto the hapless flat earthers[131] – the official narratives considered herein suffer from *blatant* deviations from scientific norms. As we have documented, they've variously kept data inputs and sources secret, excluded contrary evidence, rigged methodologies to guarantee desired outcomes, displayed extreme confirmation bias, produced conclusions that contradict their own data, been inconsistent in their justifications, and denied independent peer review. Even worse, their proponents have responded to plausible competing hypotheses with ad hominem smears and censorship in an attempt to make scientific disagreement appear to be the work of fools and idiots. In short, they have demonized dissent.

It reflects poorly on us that a principle as well established as the necessity of dissent finds itself in need of defense in the twenty-first century. Two hundred years ago John Stuart Mill understood the point very well:

> Complete liberty of contradicting and disproving our opinion is the very condition which justifies us in assuming its truth for purposes of action; and on no other terms can a being with human faculties have any rational assurance of being right.[132]

Any view will be strengthened by being challenged, because the challenge allows either a demonstration of the view's superiority or an opportunity to ameliorate its flaws. Instead of healthy competition among hypotheses, we have too often been treated to the ignominious spectacle of experienced expert scientists pleading for normal scientific debate and being vilified for their efforts.

Truth isn't established. It's dictated. Like in Orwell. We don't get analysis. We get groupthink.

It is not hyperbole to warn of a creeping authoritarianism here. The suppression of dissent by censorship and other means is one of the markers of what Umberto Eco has called Ur-Fascism, an intentionally "fuzzy" description of totalitarianism to account for its variety of manifestations. In contrast to vibrant democracies, fascist (or "Ur-Fascist") societies consider disagreement to be tantamount to treason and seek "to limit the instruments for complex and critical reasoning."[133]

At the time of this writing, calls for more censorship are increasing. When influential leaders argue for strict content "moderation" because otherwise "we lose total control,"[134] and for jailing citizens who spread social media "propaganda" favoring their political opponents,[135] we shouldn't ask first which party they're from, we should recognize these dangerous euphemisms and we should fight back. When influential leaders openly bemoan the existence of choice among news sources and refer to the First Amendment as a "major block" keeping government from "hammering" uncontrolled information "out of existence,"[136] we shouldn't look for whether it's a D or an R after their name, we should resolve to ensure that this major block keeps doing its constitutional job.

There is no greater threat to democracy than those who want to save it through censorship. Nobody has earned or ever will earn a place as arbiter of truth. Truth must be demonstrated, and it must be contestable. There aren't any trustworthy shortcuts.

Even Supreme Court Justice Oliver Wendell Holmes, the very man who originated the "fire in a crowded theater" analogy (in defense of the disgraceful, later-overturned decision in *U.S. v Schenk* that put a peaceful pamphleteer in prison), thought better of it upon reflection. In a dissenting opinion in *Abrams vs. United States*, Holmes wrote:

> The ultimate good desired is better reached by free trade in ideas
> – that the best test of truth is the power of the thought to get itself
> accepted in the competition of the market, and that truth is the
> only ground upon which their wishes safely can be carried out.[137]

No shortcuts. No taboos. No ad hominem attacks. No "total control" of information. If we don't want to employ Bertrand Russell's critical undogmatic receptiveness, what *do* we want to be? Uncritical? Dogmatic? Unreceptive?

In defense of stubborn close-mindedness, it is probably key to maintaining a secure comfort zone. It's an unflattering description of something for which it's hard to judge people too harshly. Everyone's just trying to get by. But as the kids used to say, it is what it is. Maintaining a comfort zone on the Titanic when there's still steering to be done could be considered a bit of a tragedy.

So maybe it would be good to try to train ourselves to recognize when a thought-killing stimulus has occurred, and to develop a curiosity response as a reflex. There's really nothing to lose. We can always come back to where we started if we want to.

Let me just tell you a little story and then we're out of here.

There was a kid in high school I never really liked. I didn't hate him, and I appreciated that he wasn't stupid, but he left me cold. In an earlier era, we'd have gone our separate adult ways and that would have been that. But these days, thanks to the omni-connecting tendrils of the internet, everyone ends up re-associated, and we ended up sharing some online space.

Unsurprisingly, although not without an artistic side, he'd become even more of a right-wing guy. I'd become even more lefty. Most of our views on just about everything were, and remain, diametrically opposed. The one thing we had in common was we both loved to argue. So that's what we did. Online. In front of all our former classmates. Our arguments never ended, because neither one of us knew how to stop.

He eventually managed to get the last word, but only by dying young. What a cheater.

Our early fights were bitter. However, when you want to keep fighting, the fight has to be sustainable, so we had to change tactics. First, we abandoned name-calling. That turned out to be a crucial step. Things got much better after that. Second, I stopped assuming he was evil, and he stopped assuming I was an idiot. Third, when we couldn't manage that in reality, we *pretended* to stop assuming those things. Courtesy counts. I learned these things against my will, despite my own block-headedness, through experience.

Next thing you know, we could occasionally understand things from each other's point of view – which helped us sharpen our own weapons. It raised the level of our fighting.

We didn't eliminate what was ultimately still a binary divide, but we made it considerably less absolute. We subjected it to thought and communication. We found some common ground: we were both anti-censorship, anti-authoritarian, and pro-Frank Zappa, and in those matters right and left became irrelevant. Alliances on such fundamentals are powerful, and underscore that the real world isn't cleanly divided into good-intelligent-sane and bad-stupid-loony. Or right and left. It's a profoundly human mosaic of infinite shades and combinations. By treating it as such we stood on ground simultaneously more solid and more subtle.

We did obviously become insufferable, and our classmates did kick us out of the group chat. We had to start a new one for masochists. But as annoying as we were, I think it was still better than the absolutist binary tribalism we had otherwise, which had the stale air of futility about it.

So, this book isn't asking anyone to change their positions – but maybe just to risk opening a window. We can sift through the nonsense floating around out there to find the gold simply by adhering to principles we already value. We're a democracy? We're pro-science? OK. Are we saying it or living it? Perhaps we need a splash of cold water on the face. A vigorous shaking by the shoulders. An adjustment of our comfort zones. It's time for us to be who we say we are, who we want to be. Because if we continue down the road of censorship and authoritarianism, who knows, bad things might happen. Unless you think it can't happen here.

If you agree that even one of the tabooed "lunatic" cases presented here has turned out to be worthy of more thought and discussion than our culture currently tolerates, maybe we need to change the culture. We can start with ourselves. In surreal times when it's not always clear where reality ends and madness begins, maybe it's time to take up André Breton's challenge to make of our minds a sort of laboratory "where established ideas, *no matter which*, beginning with the most elementary ones, the ones most hastily exonerated, will be accepted only for purposes of study, contingent on an examination *from top to bottom* and by definition free from all preconceptions."[138]

I've asked you to stop me if I say something crazy. Looks like you're still here.

Thank you.

ENDNOTES

1   Swanson 2023
2   Niemiec 2020
3   Johnson 2021
4   Swanson 2023
5   Kulldorff 2024
6   Othot 2023
7   Hulscher, Alexander et al. 2023
8   OIR 2024
9   Hulscher, Alexander et al. 2024
10   World Council for Health 2022
11   Bush 2001
12   Levin 2019
13   ACLU undated
14   Shir-Raz, Elisha et al. 2022
15   Greenwald 2024
16   Gerken 2024
17   Taibbi 2023
18   Kessler 2021 , Matza and Yong 2023 , Barnes 2023
19   Mordock 2024
20   Mill 2011 (1859)
21   Russell 2014 (1922)
22   Chomsky and Herman 1988
23   Marr 1996
24   Eisenhower 1961
25   Rolandsen and Selvik 2024
26   Lister 2018
27   CNN Wire Staff 2012
28   OPCW 2023
29   Maté 2023
30   Wikipedia 2018
31   Whelan 2019
32   Henderson 2020
33   Robinson 2021
34   Whelan 2019
35   Henderson 2020
36   Ibid.

37   OPCW 2019
38   Ibid.
39   Ibid.
40   Higgins 2019
41   OPCW 2020
42   Clark 2020
43   de Rivière 2021
44   Maté 2020
45   Wintour and McKernan 2020
46   NIST 2008
47   Ibid.
48   Rather 2001
49   Jowenko 2006
50   FEMA 2002
51   Glanz and Lipton 2002
52   WPI 2002
53   Glanz and Lipton 2002
54   FEMA 2002
55   NIST 2012
56   NFPA 2024
57   Abel 2008
58   NIST 2012
59   Griffin 2010
60   NIST 2008
61   NIST 2012
62   Ibid.
63   Ibid.
64   NIST 2008
65   NIST 2012
66   Hulsey 2020
67   Ibid.
68   Ibid.
69   Clark 2018
70   Aaby, Bukh et al. 1984
71   Benn, Fisker et al. 2020
72   Mogensen, Andersen et al. 2017
73   Benn 2023
74   Aaby, Mogensen et al. 2018
75   Benn, Fisker et al. 2020
76   Benn 2023

77   There was the so-called Cutter Incident involving a polio vaccine that *caused* 40,000 cases of polio that left 200 children paralyzed and 10 dead before being withdrawn; there was an inactivated measles vaccine that caused people to get much worse cases of measles, also withdrawn; there was a rotavirus vaccine that caused intussusception (bowels turning in on themselves like a folded sock) in infants until distribution was voluntarily ceased; the swine flu vaccine of 1976 was withdrawn because of

a significantly elevated rate of Guillian-Barre Syndrome in every adult age group; and the AstraZeneca Covid-19 vaccine was removed from markets "for commercial reasons" a few months after the manufacturer admitted in court that it could cause Thrombosis with Thrombocytopenia Syndrome (blood clots and low platelet counts).

78	Lazarus and Klompas 2010
79	FDA 2021
80	Kory 2023b
81	Crump and Ōmura 2011
82	Ibid.
83	Henderson and Hooper 2021
84	Agrawal and Khazaeni 2023
85	NCI 2022
86	FLCCC 2024
87	Kory 2023b
88	Ibidf.
89	Ibid.
90	Ibid.
91	Ibid.
92	Ibid.
93	Bernigaud, Guillemot et al. 2021
94	Kory 2023b
95	C19ivm 2024a
96	Lawrie 2021
97	Yagisawa, Foster et al. 2021
98	Elgazzar, Hany et al. 2020
99	Kory 2023b
100	Kory 2023b
101	Mega 2020
102	Kory 2023a
103	Ibid.
104	C19ivm 2024b
105	C19ivm 2024b
106	Kory 2024
107	Malek, Bill et al. 2021
108	NIH 2024
109	WHO 2022
110	Santi Laurini, Montanaro et al. 2022
111	Ibid.
112	WHO 2023
113	Merck 2024
114	Cohen and Kupferschmidt 2020
115	Ohl, Miller et al. 2021
116	Cohen and Kupferschmidt 2020
117	AFLN Undated
118	Mulangu, Dodd et al. 2019

119   FDA 2020

120   British Medical Journal 2020

121   British Medical Journal 2022

122   Total is sum of remdesivir figures from annual revenue reports by Gilead from 2020 to first quarter of 2024: Gilead 2021 ; Gilead 2022 ; Gilead 2023 ; Gilead 2024a ; Gilead 2024b

123   Horton 2004

124   Angell 2004

125   Relman 2002

126   Smith 2021

127   Redfield 2024

128   Union of Concerned Scientists 2017

129   Violation Tracker 2024

130   Zinn 1994

131   But I mean let's face it, if the earth were flat, cats would have knocked everything off it by now.

132   Mill 2011 (1859)

133   Eco 1995

134   Walker 2024

135   Laws 2024

136   Taibbi 2024

137   Timm 2012

138   Breton 2004 [1944]

References

Aaby, Peter, et al., 1984. "Measles vaccination and reduction in child mortality: A community study from Guinea-Bissau." *Journal of Infection* 8 (1): 13-21. https://www.sciencedirect.com/science/article/abs/pii/S016344538493192X

Aaby, Peter, et al., 2018. "Evidence of Increase in Mortality After the Introduction of Diphtheria–Tetanus–Pertussis Vaccine to Children Aged 6–35 Months in Guinea-Bissau: A Time for Reflection?" *Frontiers in Public Health* 6. https://www.frontiersin.org/journals/public-health/articles/10.3389/fpubh.2018.00079/full

Abel, Jennifer, 2008. "Theories of 9/11 (Originally published in *The Hartford Advocate*, January 29, 2008)." December 29, 2008. Retrieved May 13, 2017, from http://jenniferabel.typepad.com/jennifer_abel/2008/12/theories-of-911.html.

ACLU, undated. *Surveillance Under the Patriot Act.* American Civil Liberties Union. https://www.aclu.org/issues/national-security/privacy-and-surveillance/surveillance-under-patriot-act

AFLN, Undated. "RunDeathIsNear T-Shirt." Retrieved May 29, 2024, from https://www.americanfrontlinenurse.org/product-page/unisex-jersey-short-sleeve-tee-25.

Agrawal, Suneil and Babak Khazaeni, 2023. *Acetaminophen Toxicity.* National Institutes of Health, National Library of Medicine, National Center for Biotechnology Information.

Angell, Marcia, 2004. *The Truth About the Drug Companies: How They Deceive Us and What To Do About It.* New York: Random House.

Barnes, Julian E., 2023. "Lab Leak Most Likely Caused Pandemic, Energy Dept. Says." *The New York Times.* February 26, 2023. https://www.nytimes.com/2023/02/26/us/politics/china-lab-leak-coronavirus-pandemic.html

Benn, Christine S, 2023. On Robert F Kennedy Jr's comments on our studies of diphtheria-tetanus-pertussis vaccine. July 18, 2023. https://www.linkedin.com/pulse/robert-f-kennedy-jrs-comments-our-studies-vaccine-benn/.

Benn, Christine S, et al., 2020. "Vaccinology: time to change the paradigm?" *The Lancet Infectious Diseases* 20 (10). https://www.thelancet.com/journals/laninf/article/PIIS1473-3099(19)30742-X/abstract

Bernigaud, C., et al., 2021. "Oral ivermectin for a scabies outbreak in a long-term care facility: potential value in preventing COVID-19 and associated mortality." *Br J Dermatol* 184 (6): 1207-1209.

Breton, André, 2004 [1944]. *Arcanum 17*. Los Angeles: Green Integer. Zack Rogow, translator.

British Medical Journal, 2020. WHO Guideline Development Group advises against use of remdesivir for covid-19. https://www.bmj.com/company/newsroom/who-guideline-development-group-advises-against-use-of-remdesivir-for-covid-19/

British Medical Journal, 2022. Update to living WHO guideline on drugs for covid-19. https://www.bmj.com/content/378/bmj.o2224

Bush, George W., 2001. "President Bush Addresses the Nation [full text of his public address to a Joint Session of Congress]." *Washington Post*. September 20, 2001. http://www.washingtonpost.com/wp-srv/nation/specials/attacked/transcripts/bushaddress_092001.html

C19ivm, 2024a. "Covid 19 Treatment Research: Ivermectin." from https://c19ivm.org/.

C19ivm, 2024b. "Ivermectin PRINCIPLE Late Treatment RCT." Retrieved May 29, 2024, from https://c19ivm.org/principleivm.html.

Chomsky, Noam and Edward S. Herman, 1988. *Manufacturing Consent: The Political Economy of the Mass Media*. New York: Knopf Doubleday.

Clark, Daniel J., 2018. *Behind the Curve*. Delta-V Productions.

Clark, Kelly, 2020. *Remarks at a UN Security Council Arria-Formula Meeting on Chemical Weapons in Syria*. https://2017-2021-translations.state.gov/2020/09/28/remarks-at-a-un-security-council-arria-formula-meeting-on-chemical-weapons-in-syria-via-vtc/

CNN Wire Staff, 2012. "Obama warns Syria not to cross 'red line.'" *CNN*. August 21, 2012. https://edition.cnn.com/2012/08/20/world/meast/syria-unrest/index.html

Cohen, Jon and Kai Kupferschmidt, 2020. "The 'very, very bad look' of remdesivir, the first FDA-approved COVID-19 drug." *Science* October 28, 2020.

Crump, A. and S. Ōmura, 2011. "Ivermectin, 'wonder drug' from Japan: the human use perspective." *Proc Jpn Acad Ser B Phys Biol Sci* 87 (2): 13-28.

de Rivière, Nicolas, 2021. *Statement by Mr. Nicolas de Rivière, permanent representative of France to the United Nations - UN Security Council Arria formula meeting*. https://fr.franceintheus.org/spip.php?article10239

Eco, Umberto, 1995. "Ur-Fascism." *New York Review of Books*. June 22, 1995.

Eisenhower, Dwight, 1961. *President Eisenhower's Farewell Address.* https://www.archives.gov/milestone-documents/president-dwight-d-eisenhowers-farewell-address

Elgazzar, Ahmed, et al., 2020. "Efficacy and Safety of Ivermectin for Treatment and prophylaxis of COVID-19 Pandemic." *Research Square.* https://doi.org/10.21203/rs.3.rs-100956/v2

FDA, 2020. *Coronavirus (COVID-19) Update: FDA Issues Emergency Use Authorization for Potential COVID-19 Treatment.* Food and Drug Administration. https://www.fda.gov/news-events/press-announcements/coronavirus-covid-19-update-fda-issues-emergency-use-authorization-potential-covid-19-treatment

FDA, 2021. *Tweet, August 21, 2021: Why You Should Not Use Ivermectin to Treat or Prevent COVID-19.*

FEMA, 2002. *World Trade Center Building Performance Study.* Federal Emergency Management Agency. https://www.fema.gov/media-library/assets/documents/3544

FLCCC, 2024. "Front Line Critical Covid Care Alliance." from https://covid19criticalcare.com/.

Gerken, Tom, 2024. "Zuckerberg regrets bowing to Biden 'pressure' over Covid." *BBC News.* https://www.bbc.co.uk/news/articles/czxlpjlgdzjo

Gilead, 2021. Gilead Sciences Announces Fourth Quarter and Full Year 2020 Financial Results. https://www.gilead.com/news-and-press/press-room/press-releases/2021/2/gilead-sciences-announces-fourth-quarter-and-full-year-2020-financial-results

Gilead, 2022. *Gilead Sciences Announces Fourth Quarter and Full Year 2021 Financial Results.* https://www.gilead.com/news-and-press/press-room/press-releases/2022/2/gilead-sciences-announces-fourth-quarter-and-full-year-2021-financial-results

Gilead, 2023. *Gilead Sciences Announces Fourth Quarter and Full Year 2022 Financial Results.* https://www.gilead.com/news-and-press/press-room/press-releases/2023/2/gilead-sciences-announces-fourth-quarter-and-full-year-2022-financial-results

Gilead, 2024a. Gilead Sciences Announces First Quarter 2024 Financial Results. https://www.gilead.com/news-and-press/press-room/press-releases/2024/4/gilead-sciences-announces-first-quarter-2024-financial-results

Gilead, 2024b. Gilead Sciences Announces Fourth Quarter and Full Year 2023 Financial Results. https://www.gilead.com/news-and-press/press-room/press-releases/2024/2/gilead-sciences-announces-fourth-quar-ter-and-full-year-2023-financial-results

Glanz, James and Eric Lipton, 2002. "A Search for Clues in Towers' Collapse." *The New York Times*. February 2, 2002.

Greenwald, Glenn, 2024. SCOTUS Protects Biden Administration's Social Media Censorship Program from Review. *Video Transcript*. https://greenwald.locals.com/post/5804293/cnn-s-kasie-hunt-has-humiliating-meltdown-ahead-of-biden-trump-debate-scotus-protects-biden-admin.

Griffin, David Ray, 2010. "Building What? How SCADs Can Be Hidden in Plain Sight." *Foreign Policy Journal*. May 31, 2010. https://www.foreignpolicyjournal.com/2010/05/31/building-what-how-scads-can-be-hidden-in-plain-sight/

Henderson, David R. and Charles L. Hooper, 2021. "Why Is the FDA Attacking a Safe, Effective Drug?" *The Wall Street Journal*. July 28, 2021. https://www.wsj.com/articles/fda-ivermectin-covid-19-coronavirus-masks-anti-science-11627482393

Henderson, Ian, 2020. *Statement to a Meeting during the OPCW Conference of States Parties*. https://thegrayzone.com/wp-content/uploads/2020/02/Henderson-Testimony-UN.pdf

Higgins, Elliot, 2019. Consecutive tweets. https://twitter.com/EliotHiggins/status/1129398851725664256

Horton, Richard, 2004. "The Dawn of McScience." *New York Review of Books* 51:7.

Hulscher, Nicolas, et al., 2023. A Systematic Review of Autopsy Findings in Deaths after COVID-19 Vaccination. Preprints with The Lancet. https://papers.ssrn.com/sol3/papers.cfm?abstract_id=4496137

Hulscher, Nicolas, et al., 2024. "A systematic review of autopsy findings in deaths after Covid-19 vaccination." *Forensic Science International*: 112115. https://www.sciencedirect.com/science/article/pii/S0379073824001968

Hulsey, J. Leroy, Quan, Zhili, Xiao, Feng, 2020. *A Structural Reevaluation of the Collapse of World Trade Center 7*. University of Alaska Fairbanks, Department of Civil and Environmental Engineering. University of Alaska Fairbanks. March 2020. https://files.wtc7report.org/file/public-download/A-Structural-Reevaluation-of-the-Collapse-of-World-Trade-Center-7-March2020.pdf

Johnson, Ron, 2021. "YouTube Cancels the U.S. Senate." *Wall Street Journal*. February 2, 2021. https://www.wsj.com/articles/youtube-cancels-the-u-s-senate-11612288061

Jowenko, Danny, 2006. Dutch Journalist Interviews Demolition Expert Danny Jowenko. https://www.youtube.com/watch?v=ixoE8K484oY

Kessler, Glenn, 2021. "Timeline: How the Wuhan lab-leak theory suddenly became credible." *Washington Post.* May 25, 2021. https://www.washingtonpost.com/politics/2021/05/25/timeline-how-wuhan-lab-leak-theory-suddenly-became-credible/

Kory, Pierre, 2023a. Chapter Twenty-Five: Counterfeit Trials — The Big Six. *The War on Ivermectin: The Medicine that Saved Millions and Could Have Ended the Pandemic.* New York: Skyhorse Publishing.

Kory, Pierre, 2023b. *The War on Ivermectin: The Medicine that Saved Millions and Could Have Ended the Pandemic.* New York: Skyhorse Publishing.

Kory, Pierre, 2024. The Last of The "Big Seven" Fraudulent Ivermectin Trials Has Finally Been Published. *Pierre Kory's Medical Musings.* March 5, 2024. https://pierrekorymedicalmusings.com/p/the-last-of-the-big-seven-fraudulent.

Kulldorff, Martin, 2024. "Harvard Tramples the Truth." *City Journal.* https://www.city-journal.org/article/harvard-tramples-the-truth

Lawrie, Theresa Anne, 2021. *Written Evidence Submitted by Dr Theresa Anne Lawrie, Director, The Evidence-Based Medicine Consultancy Ltd.* Coronavirus: Lessons Learnt, Health and Social Care Committee, UK Parliament. https://committees.parliament.uk/writtenevidence/36858/pdf/

Laws, Jasmine, 2024. "Hillary Clinton Suggests Posting Russian Propaganda Should Be A Crime." *Newsweek.* September 17, 2024. https://www.newsweek.com/hillary-clinton-spreading-russian-misinformation-crime-1954941

Lazarus, Ross and Michael Klompas, 2010. *Electronic Support for Public Health - Vaccine Adverse Event Reporting System (ESP:VAERS).* Harvard Pilgrim Health Care, for the Agency for Healthcare Research and Quality (AHRQ), US Department of Health and Human Services (HHS). https://digital.ahrq.gov/sites/default/files/docs/publication/r18hs017045-lazarus-final-report-2011.pdf

Levin, Sam, 2019. "Revealed: FBI Investigated Civil Rights Group As 'Terrorism' Threat And Viewed KKK As Victims." *The Guardian.* February 1, 2019. https://www.theguardian.com/us-news/2019/feb/01/sacramento-rally-fbi-kkk-domestic-terrorism-california

Lister, Tim, 2018. "Assad may win Syria's war, but he will preside over a broken country." *CNN.* March 15, 2018. https://www.cnn.com/2018/03/15/middleeast/assad-the-victor-tim-lister-intl/index.html

Malek, Rory J., et al., 2021. "Clinical drug therapies and biologicals currently used or in clinical trial to treat COVID-19." *Biomedicine & Pharmacotherapy* 144 (December 2021). https://www.sciencedirect.com/science/article/pii/S075333222101060X

Marr, Andrew, 1996. "Interview with Noam Chomsky." *The Big Idea (BBC)*. February 1996. https://www.youtube.com/watch?v=GjENnyQupow&t=557s

Maté, Aaron, 2020. "OPCW Syria Whistleblower and Ex-Director Attacked by US, UK, France at UN." *The Grayzone*. October 7, 2020. https://thegrayzone.com/2020/10/07/opcw-syria-whistleblower-and-ex-opcw-chief-attacked-by-us-uk-french-at-un/

Maté, Aaron, 2023. "Burying key evidence, new OPCW report covers up Douma's unsolved deaths." *The Grayzone*. March 27, 2023. https://thegrayzone.com/2023/03/27/burying-key-evidence-new-opcw-report-covers-up-doumas-unsolved-deaths/

Matza, Max and Nicholas Yong, 2023. "FBI chief Christopher Wray says China lab leak most likely." *BBC News*. March 1, 2023. https://www.bbc.co.uk/news/world-us-canada-64806903

Mega, E.R., 2020. "Latin America's embrace of an unproven COVID treatment is hindering drug trials." *Nature* 586 (7830): 481-482.

Merck, 2024. *Merck Announces Fourth-Quarter and Full-Year 2023 Financial Results*. https://www.merck.com/news/merck-announces-fourth-quarter-and-full-year-2023-financial-results/

Mill, John Stuart, 2011 (1859). *On Liberty*. London: Project Gutenberg (Originally John W. Parker and Son). https://www.gutenberg.org/files/34901/34901-h/34901-h.htm

Mogensen, Soren Wengel, et al., 2017. "The Introduction of Diphtheria-Tetanus-Pertussis and Oral Polio Vaccine Among Young Infants in an Urban African Community: A Natural Experiment." *EBioMedicine* 17: 192-198. https://www.thelancet.com/action/showPdf?pii=S2352-3964%2817%2930046-4

Mordock, Jeff, 2024. "FBI agent confirms authenticity of Hunter Biden's laptop." *The Washington Times*. June 4, 2024. https://www.washingtontimes.com/news/2024/jun/4/erika-jensen-confirms-authenticity-of-hunter-biden/

Mulangu, Sabue, et al., 2019. "A Randomized, Controlled Trial of Ebola Virus Disease Therapeutics." *New England Journal of Medicine* 381 (24): 2293-2303. https://www.nejm.org/doi/full/10.1056/NEJMoa1910993

NCI, 2022. *Off-Label Drug Use in Cancer Treatment*. https://www.cancer.gov/about-cancer/treatment/drugs/off-label

NFPA, 2024. *NFPA 921: Guide for Fire and Explosion Investigations*. National Fire Protection Association. https://www.nfpa.org/codes-and-standards/nfpa-921-standard-development/921

Niemiec, Emilia, 2020. "COVID-19 and misinformation." *EMBO reports* 21 (11): e51420. https://doi.org/10.15252/embr.202051420

NIH, 2024. *NIH Covid Treatment Guidelines: Molnupiravir.* National Institutes of Health. https://www.covid19treatmentguidelines.nih.gov/therapies/antivirals-including-antibody-products/molnupiravir/

NIST, 2008. *Final Report on the Collapse of World Trade Center Building 7, Federal Building and Fire Safety Investigation of the World Trade Center Disaster (NIST NCSTAR 1A).* National Institute for Standards and Technology. November 20, 2008. https://www.nist.gov/publications/final-report-collapse-world-trade-center-building-7-federal-building-and-fire-safety-0

NIST, 2012. "FAQs: NIST WTC7 Investigation." June 27, 2012. Retrieved May 12, 2017, from https://www.nist.gov/el/faqs-nist-wtc-7-investigation.

Ohl, Michael E., et al., 2021. "Association of Remdesivir Treatment With Survival and Length of Hospital Stay Among US Veterans Hospitalized With COVID-19." *JAMA Network Open* 4 (7): e2114741-e2114741. https://doi.org/10.1001/jamanetworkopen.2021.14741

OIR, 2024. "Observatory of International Research." from https://ooir.org/.

OPCW, 2019. *Report of the OPCW Fact-Finding Mission in Syria Regarding the Incident of Alleged Use of Toxic Chemicals as a Weapon in Douma, Syrian Arab Republic, On 7 April 2018.* Organization for the Prohibition of Chemical Weapons. https://www.opcw.org/sites/default/files/documents/2019/03/s-1731-2019%28e%29.pdf

OPCW, 2020. *Director-General's Statement on the Report of the Investigation into Possible Breaches of Confidentiality.* February 6, 2020. https://www.opcw.org/sites/default/files/documents/2020/02/OPCW%20Director-General's%20Statement%20on%20the%20Report%20of%20the%20Investigation%20into%20Possible%20Breaches%20of%20Confidentiality.pdf

OPCW, 2023. OPCW Releases Third Report by Investigation and Identification Team. https://www.opcw.org/media-centre/news/2023/01/opcw-releases-third-report-investigation-and-identification-team

Othot, Seamus, 2023. "Dr. Meryl Nass, Top Critic of Mills' COVID Policies, Sees Medical License Suspension Extended." *The Maine Wire.* December 15, 2023. https://www.themainewire.com/2023/12/dr-meryl-nass-top-critic-of-mills-covid-policies-sees-medical-license-suspension-extended/

Rather, Dan, 2001. "Dan Rather Reports Live on WTC7 Collapse for CBS News." September 11, 2001. Retrieved May 12, 2017, from https://www.youtube.com/watch?v=Nvx904dAw0o.

Redfield, Robert, 2024. "Donald Trump Has a Plan to Make America's Children Healthy Again. It's a Good One." *Newsweek.* September 24, 2024.

Relman, Arthur, 2002. "America's Other Drug Problem." *New Republic* December 16:27.

Robinson, Piers, 2021. *The OPCW Douma Investigation: Manipulation of Key Toxicology and Related Information Regarding Alleged Victims between the Original Interim Report and the Final Report.* Working Group on Syria, Propaganda and Media. December 2021. https://syriapropagandamedia.org/1200-2

Rolandsen, Øystein H. and Kjetil Selvik, 2024. "Disposable rebels: US military assistance to insurgents in the Syrian war." *Mediterranean Politics* 29 (4): 528-549. https://doi.org/10.1080/13629395.2023.2183664

Russell, Bertrand, 2014 (1922). *Free Thought and Official Propaganda.* Project Gutenberg.

Santi Laurini, G., et al., 2022. "Safety Profile of Molnupiravir in the Treatment of COVID-19: A Descriptive Study Based on FAERS Data." *J Clin Med* 12 (1).

Shir-Raz, Y., et al., 2022. "Censorship and Suppression of Covid-19 Heterodoxy: Tactics and Counter-Tactics." *Minerva*: 1-27.

Smith, Richard, 2021. Time to assume that health research is fraudulent until proved otherwise? *Richard Smith's Non-Medical Blogs.* July 2, 2021. https://richardswsmith.wordpress.com/2021/07/02/time-to-assume-that-health-research-is-fraudulent-until-proved-otherwise/.

Swanson, Bret, 2023. "Covid Censorship Proved To Be Deadly." *The Washington Post.* July 7, 2023. https://www.wsj.com/articles/covid-censorship-proved-to-be-deadly-social-media-government-pandemic-health-697c32c4

Taibbi, Matt, 2023. The Censorship-Industrial Complex. *The Twitter Files.* March 9, 2023. https://twitterfiles.substack.com/p/the-censorship-industrial-complex.

Taibbi, Matt, 2024. "Walter Kirn's "Rescue The Republic" Speech (Transcript)." *Racket News.* October 1, 2024. https://www.racket.news/p/walter-kirns-rescue-the-republic

Timm, Trevor, 2012. "It's Time to Stop Using the 'Fire in a Crowded Theater' Quote." *The Atlantic.* November 2, 2012. https://www.theatlantic.com/national/archive/2012/11/its-time-to-stop-using-the-fire-in-a-crowded-theater-quote/264449/

Union of Concerned Scientists, 2017. "The Disinformation Playbook Case Study: GlaxoSmithKline Tried to Silence the Scientist Who Exposed the Dangers of its Drug Avandia." from https://www.ucsusa.org/resources/glaxosmithkline-tried-silence-scientist-who-exposed-dangers-its-drug-avandia.

Violation Tracker, 2024. *Pharmaceutical Industry Violations.* https://violationtracker.goodjobsfirst.org/industry/pharmaceuticals

Walker, Jackson, 2024. "Hillary Clinton warns 'we lose total control' without social media content moderation." *CBS News.* October 7, 2024. https://cbsaustin.com/news/nation-world/hillary-clinton-warns-we-lose-total-control-without-social-media-content-moderation-politics-facebook-x-twitter-tiktok-meta-section-230

Whelan, Brendan, 2019. "Letter to OPCW Director General Fernando Arias." from https://thegrayzone.com/wp-content/uploads/2020/10/BW-Letter-to-DG-April-2019-Redacted-GZ.pdf.

WHO, 2022. *WHO updates its treatment guidelines to include molnupiravir.* World Health Organization. https://www.who.int/news/item/03-03-2022-molnupiravir

WHO, 2023. *WHO updates guidelines on treatments for COVID-19.* World Health Organization. https://www.who.int/news/item/10-11-2023-who-updates-guidelines-on-treatments-for-covid-19

Wikipedia, 2018. "Douma Chemical Attack." Retrieved April 14, 2024, from https://en.wikipedia.org/wiki/Douma_chemical_attack.

Wintour, Patrick and Bethan McKernan, 2020. "Inquiry Strikes Blow to Russian Denials of Syria Chemical Attack." *The Guardian.* February 7, 2020. https://www.theguardian.com/world/2020/feb/07/inquiry-strikes-blow-to-russian-denials-of-syria-chemical-attack

World Council for Health, 2022. "World Council for Health Stands with Dr Peter A. McCullough, MD, MPH." from https://worldcouncilforhealth.org/news/statements/peter-mccullough/

WPI, 2002. "The "Deep Mystery" of Melted Steel." *WPI Transformations* (Spring 2002). http://www.wpi.edu/News/Transformations/2002Spring/steel.html

Yagisawa, Morimasa, et al., 2021. "Global trends in clinical studies of ivermectin in COVID-19." *The Japanese Journal of Antibiotics* 74 (1). https://www.antibiotics.or.jp/wp-content/uploads/74-1_44-95.pdf

Zinn, Howard, 1994. *You Can't Be Neutral on a Moving Train: A Personal History of Our Times.* Boston: Beacon Press.